MW01488244

CENTRAL

ON THE CHURCH IN THE 21ST CENTURY

THOUGHTS

Essays from the Faculty of Central Baptist Theological Seminary

For
Chuck and Sue
and
Dick and Anne-Marie

Best wishes,
David Wheeler

220
Cli

CENTRAL

ON THE CHURCH IN THE 21ST CENTURY

THOUGHTS

Essays from the Faculty of Central Baptist Theological Seminary

THOMAS E. CLIFTON
EDITOR

SMYTH&HELWYS
PUBLISHING, INCORPORATED   MACON, GEORGIA

ISBN 1-57312-172-X

Central Thoughts on the Church in the 21st Century

Thomas E. Clifton, Editor

Copyright © 1998

Smyth & Helwys Publishing, Inc.
6316 Peake Road
Macon, Georgia 31210-3960
1-800-747-3016

All rights reserved.
Printed in the United States of America.

The paper used in this publication meets the minimum requirements of
American National Standard for Printed Library Materials,
ANSI Z39.48–1984.

Library of Congress Cataloguing-in-Publication Data

Central thoughts on the church in the 21st century/
    Thomas E. Clifton, editor.
    p.   cm.
    Includes bibliographical references.
    ISBN 1-57312-172-X   (alk. paper)
    1. Church—Forecasting.
    2. Twenty-first century—Forecasts.
    3. Baptists—United States—Forecasting.
    I. Clifton, Thomas.
    BV600.2.C42   1998
    270'.0905—dc21

          98-16755
          CIP

Contents

FIRST THOUGHTS

AN INTRODUCTION

Thomas E. Clifton

I HAVE NEVER BEEN GOOD AT PREDICTING THE FUTURE or knowing which newly arrived fashions were permanent. The first prediction I recall making, with considerable confidence, was the presidential election of 1952. I was ten years old, living in a small Missouri town. The election pitted Governor Adlai Stevenson of Illinois against the smiling Ike, General Dwight David Eisenhower. The GOP in my home county was so weak that candidates didn't even file for most elected positions. With rare exceptions, a Democrat held every elected office in the county. As I listened around the kitchen table to the election talk that went on that fall, it was clear to me that there was no way General Eisenhower was going to win. All of my relatives were voting for Governor Stevenson—and so was everyone else in my small world.

I woke on the November Wednesday after election day in 1952 to discover that Ike had defeated and beat our beloved Adlai by a resounding 442–89 electoral votes. When I learned that even Missouri had sided with the winner, my confidence as a predictor was shaken. Actually, it was more than that. For the first time I glimpsed life's unpredictability. And I realized that the small world I inhabited in Crystal City, Missouri, was an inadequate measuring stick for knowing the rest of the world. Few times in my life have I felt more disoriented or more confused.

Since then, of course, I have been wrong about an amazing number of things. When longer hair on men became fashionable, I predicted that the flat-top was extinct—but now I see a short-haired species of young kids everywhere again. When cities across the country began building new stadiums for baseball and football back in the 60s, I predicted the demise of spectator sports and insisted that the money was being wasted—but now, even Cleveland fills the bleachers for baseball. When television started broadcasting news 24 hours a day, I recoiled with disbelief—who would want to watch the news before or after 6:00 P.M.?—but now we demand around-the-clock news to keep abreast of the latest scandal or war.

Failure to anticipate the future has wreacked havoc in many lives. Mark Twain had a chance to invest in the telephone in its embryonic stages but passed it up for a number of silly ideas that never got off the ground. Gary Cooper turned down the chance to play the leading role in *Gone With the Wind* because he believed the whole project would fall flat on its face. In 1977, the CEO of Digital Equipment publicly pronounced that there is no reason anyone would want a home computer. And we all know that in 1899, the U.S. Office of Patents confidently announced that everything possible to be invented had already been invented. The list of lost opportunities and miscalculations by people who should have known better is legion.

How can any of us know what to expect next? Surely shocks and surprises are just around the corner. Do we have any idea what is in store for us as the 21st century welcomes us? Even the Bible cautions us about attempting to get too far ahead of ourselves:

> Come now, you who say, "Today or tomorrow we will go to such and such a town and spend a year there, doing business and making money." Yet you do not even know what tomorrow will bring. (Jas 4:13-14a)

Is there any verse in the Bible that rings truer? Speaking about the future requires that we wear a very humble spirit. Overconfidence can make any of us look foolish.

We do expect that the 21st century will accelerate the changes we have already experienced. When my mother attended elementary grades, her means of transportation to a country school involved riding a horse partway, taking a canoe across a creek, and walking the remaining distance. She was born in the 20th century, but the jet plane, the television, and the home computer existed only in the imaginations of a few. How can we even begin to imagine the road ahead? Where do we find the clues, keeping in mind that we cannot see through this glass clearly?

Frankly, many of us are not keen about the future, and if you are one of them, don't feel alone. Some scary things hide under the rocks that we have to clear in the path called the 21st century. No wonder that fear and apprehension stalk the land. No wonder that home schooling has taken hold. No wonder that hate groups are entrenched. No wonder that street gangs roam the cities. No wonder that gated communities and private police protection dot the land. All of these things and more tell us that the 21st century has dark clouds not only on the far horizon but directly overhead. *The Christian Century* magazine took that name in 1900, having been founded in 1884 under a different title. Such hope and optimism are not ours. We are less sure about almost everything in our postmodern situation. (For a fuller treatment of this theme, read David Wheeler's chapter, which unpacks the theological and philosophical earthquakes that make our new century a much different situation for Christian faith.)

Surely part of our fear about the 21st century is that it has come too soon. We have not yet adjusted to the changes of the 20th century. Peter Drucker, in a 1994 article in *The Atlantic Monthly,* reflected: "No century in recorded history has experienced so many social transformations and such radical ones as the 20th century."[1] Here, Drucker delineates what we have already suspected: the 20th century was probably the cruelest ever with its wars and holocausts. Drucker helps us understand why we feel so terribly stressed and so emotionally frayed: "Far smaller and far slower social changes in earlier periods triggered civil wars, rebellions, and violent intellectual and spiritual crisis."[2]

You and I have been living through change at a faster rate than any human beings in any previous time. No other people in the long history of the race have endured what we have just experienced. In earlier centuries, several generations were given time to adjust to very small changes. Now, major changes seem to barrage us. Little wonder that our social problems seem so massive and our personal struggles often feel so hopeless.

Our human failures in the 20th century are remarkable. No other epoch in the history of the world has come close to matching the pace of change we have just lived through. The lives around us that have been wounded or destroyed by drugs, brutalized by senseless violence, or devastated by sexual experimentation point not only to the failure of personal responsibility; but they also point to the social chaos caused by change that is greater than we can bear. In light of what we have gone through as a society, it is only by grace that any of us make it at all. And it is not surprising that most of us have people in our immediate family or local congregation who have broken under the pressure. Divorce, suicide, abortion, eating disorders, emotional distress—who among us has not been affected and wounded? Too much change. Too fast.

So if you were naming a new magazine for the 21st century, what would you call it? I might be tempted to call it *Survival,* but that sounds too much like some supremacists in the woods, prisoners of hate and fear. The other part of me wants to name it *Don't Worry, Be Happy* in the realization that none of us can do very much to alter things—what will be will be, after all. The better part of me is between those two extremes. I cannot force the world to be what I want. But neither can I accept the world as it happens. A response to the 21st century that is faithful to God requires acceptance at some points and work for radical change at other points. In the words of the familiar prayer, may God help us change those things that can and should be changed, grant us strength to accept what cannot be changed, and wisdom to know the difference.

So I return to my beginning. I have often failed to predict the future. I recognize that others, far more astute than I, have also failed to make wise predictions. And I am most mindful that the Bible cautions us against presuming to know the future. Nevertheless, I am going to skate out on this thin ice. My faculty colleagues at Central Baptist Theological Seminary join me in this caper. Each of them has attempted to speak a relevant word from the perspective of their chosen field. How do we read the Bible, how do we preach and worship, where is renewal of stewardship, how do we counter postmodern challenges to belief?—these and other issues are explored. By examining an issue, each of the writers provides a vital transition to the new century. These chapters do not spell out details—that is thin ice indeed. Rather, they challenge us to develop the tools that will enable us to cope with some rather turbulent times.

So what changes do I foresee?

(1) *I think the 21st century will nail the lid shut on denominationalism as we have known it in this century.* That is hardly a new thought. Experts have been saying this for some time. I don't believe denominations will disappear any more than the high school reunion will. It is just that few people care much anymore about either one. When I was growing up, denominations really did provide a sense of identity. We knew who we were and who we were not by our church identity. It really was a matter of concern if a Baptist girl or boy married someone outside the faith—such as a Lutheran or a Presbyterian. And a Baptist who married a Roman Catholic would send the entire congregation to its knees and create a lifelong family crisis. Today most parents just hope their children will attend church—any church. In our mobile society the new church of choice when people relocate is inevitably up for grabs. This is not new.

We will continue to see, I suspect, fluid-denominational identity. Denominations will continue to do the things people need, such as provide retirement programs and ordination tracks. But the 20th-century model of denominational life, where one denomination provides literally everything from hymnals, bulletins, offering envelopes, missionaries, church camp, college, seminary, and retirement home—to list only a few services—is over.

The key factor is quality. Churches will respond to the denomination or independent vendor that provides the level of quality that fits the church's interest, taste, and needs. This is something to accept. The resources in any one denomination to produce and support everything from A to Z are absent. Quality will almost always win a following.

Not only will resources be in flux, but also entire denominations will reconfigure. Some denominations, such as the Disciples of Christ and the United Church of Christ, have already forged a working partnership. Discussions between Episcopalians and Lutherans will certainly resume and will create an early 21st-century model for denominational unity between very different communions. Other denominations are grappling internally. Presbyterians and Methodists have lost millions of members in the late 20th century. This hemorrhage is not over by a long shot. The mainline congregations I visit are predominately made up of people 60 years and older. With such statistics, it is uncertain how many houses of worship will remain open twenty years from now, miracles not withstanding. Not long ago Daniel Aleshire, executive director of the Association of Theological Schools, remarked that we can no longer talk meaningfully about denominations. Rather, we must view congregation by congregation. Some mainline congregations may be thriving, but their denominations are in free fall, Aleshire concluded.

The situation is so fluid among Baptists that even insiders struggle to understand what's happening. Pity the non-Baptist who tries to understand! Some Baptist state conventions in the South have rival organizations—moderates and conservatives. The issue of homosexuality has exposed all the divisions within American Baptists, the nation's most racially and ethnically diverse denomination. National Baptists struggle to reform a system in which leaders are occasionally unaccountable and in which change toward inclusion of women and young leaders has been slow in coming.

My own denominational journey has been Baptist in both south and north. I was born in a border state and have been a border Baptist. I was licensed to preach in a Southern Baptist church and ordained in an American Baptist church. Today I might preach in Arkansas one Sunday and Minnesota the next. The seminary I serve is committed to the whole family of Baptists, especially American Baptists and Cooperative Baptists. Central Baptist Theological Seminary finds its mission on the "border" to bring together Baptists who love one another together.

I would like to invite others to join us in the effort. The Civil War that divided us is over and has been for some time now. The game of narrow denominationalism is over and will not serve us well in the 21st century. If the Episcopalians and Lutherans can recognize each other's ordinations, is there reason to do less among equally qualified Baptists who want to cooperate across established lines of division? The Green Lake Conference Center in Wisconsin has emerged as a national assembly place for all Baptists. The Ministers and Missionaries Board of the American Baptist Churches now serves various Baptist entities. Smyth & Helwys Publishing in Macon, Georgia, and the Baptist Center for Ethics in Nashville, Tennessee, are eager to serve Baptists nationwide. The Baptist Joint Committee, the Baptist Peace Fellowship, and the Baptist World Alliance all represent and serve varied Baptist entities.

I foresee Baptists in the North and South continuing to have family reunions at national and state or regional levels in the 21st century. But I envision a growing partnership between two mission boards, one in Atlanta and one in Valley Forge. I strongly covet for Cooperative Baptists the vital witness that ethnic minorities bring to the table and that has so long been part of American Baptist life. Right now both American Baptists and Cooperative Baptists have much that is positive to offer one another. I hope we will not squander the opportunity for a real partnership in the 21st century.

Since I am already on thin ice here, I may as well skate on. Since Valley Forge seems to have become a stumbling block for many American Baptists, a task force is presently reviewing the whole denominational question for ABCUSA. Some have suggested selling the valuable real estate in Pennsylvania and relocating administrative and program offices to Green Lake or another more central location. Such restructuring would release new energies for evangelism and missions as well as create wider opportunities for Baptist partnerships. Skeptics might then acknowledge that we really are more interested in winning people to Christ and doing kingdom business among the poor than in intramural scrimmage.

One final note about denominations, and one hope for a particular denomination. The Roman Catholic Church is a sleeping giant on the American scene. It is breathtaking to consider the spiritual resources that would be unleashed if the Catholic Church in America recognized a married clergy, affirmed women priests, and accepted modern methods of birth control. It is hard to imagine any of these changes occurring unless the Roman Catholic Church in America becomes a national church, and no one I've ever talked to believes this will happen. If it does not happen, we are all the poorer. A revival of faith and witness among Catholics is exactly what all Christians need in the 21st century. Having grown up Southern Baptist near

St. Louis, when Catholics were the identified enemy, it is ironic that I now pray for a Catholic revival. But then, this is the 21st century.

(2) *Science and technology will usher unprecedented upheavals into our lives.* That is a safe prediction. It has already happened. "Dolly" has been cloned. What next? Since the lid of Pandora's Box has been blown off in the science lab, the question about what kind of human beings we are going to become in the 21st century is infinitely more complex, decidedly more uncertain. Doing evangelism and Christian education will be quite a challenge indeed.

Technology has altered our use of time. Technology has given us more leisure time, one hour more every day than we had even as recently as 1965. Some people have used this time to exercise, attend continuing education classes, read books like this one, and pursue a host of other interests. However, many other people have used this extra hour a day to watch more television. If you are average, you will watch 16 hours of television a week, an increase of 4 hours from what you watched in 1965. Many newer homes are even being built with a theater for home viewing.

Technology has also altered our sense of time. What we are viewing comes to us faster than ever. We must have our remote control to change quickly from channel to channel. Channel-changing addicts, called "surfers," switch channels 22 times a minute. Commercials, as you have probably noticed, often combine 20 or 30 different shots in as many seconds. Because of the speed of television, children growing up today are different. They see and think and process information differently than children of previous generations.

Not only is the media producing a different kind of learner; the media is also creating values. I would rather say that our values come from church and family. I would rather say that values are learned in the laps of our grandmothers who read us stories after school. I would rather say that values are learned in school where good teachers probe and challenge students toward the meaning of truth, honesty, and justice.

To some extent values are being learned in the home, in the church, in the school, and in institutions such as Boy Scouts that stress character. But let's face it: we are way behind the leader. Values today are learned from commercials, music, television, and the cinema. It is not surprising that America's number one export to the world is not grain from Kansas or automobiles from Michigan or wine from California. Our best export is the American movie. Human behavior is being shaped by electronic media, and our traditional institutions have not significantly adapted nor influenced it.

We cannot expect the power of electronic technology to lessen in the 21st century.

Envisioning change through technology has been the lifelong quest of Arthur Clarke who gave us *2001: A Space Odyssey*. Back in 1945, still in his twenties, Clark wrote about communication satellites in space, anticipating by several years the technology we now take for granted. Scientists read Clarke and made his science fiction come true. Now Clarke has given us a new vision of the future in *3001: The Final Odyssey*. In this future no one will have to go to school or take training, for we will have the "brain cap." The brain cap downloads all the knowledge and skills required to reach full potential. In such a world, religion is evil and irrational—even though the idea of God persists. After all, why is religion needed? Those inclined toward evil can be reprogrammed by the brain cap.

Even now scientists who are working on brain research have come up with some startling conclusions and in the process have created new controversies about how free we really are to make decisions. The process, called brain imaging, is found among those who practice neuroscience, perhaps the hottest field in the academic world today.

Already scientists have developed an IQ Cap. It works very simply and takes only 15 minutes to adjust and a mere 16 seconds to run. There is no pain and no cutting of hair, just messing it up a little. The cap is supposed to track brain waves that provide an exact reading of IQ without any cultural bias.

The concept of an IQ Cap may sound harmless, but research in neuroscience has gone beyond IQ testing. Brain research has convinced neuroscientists that we are all genetically wired through our evolutionary history in certain ways and that there is very little we can do about it. Our happiness is genetically determined. The fat content of our body is genetically determined. In fact, there seems to be little about any of us that isn't fixed in the brain.

These scientists are just not whistling in the dark. They are able to use scanner screens that show when certain genes light up inside the brain resulting from specific behaviors or preferences. The more these scientists see and probe, the more convinced they become that our temperament, emotions, moral choices, and the roles we play in life have little to do with choice. We are wired from the start of life. Thus, some of us are wired to become Mother Teresa. And some of us are wired to become killers. There is no free will. There are no choices. There is no self-control. There is, in the end, no self. Everything about us is genetically determined.

Arthur Clarke's fictional brain cap programs people according to potential. With current brain scanners, people are seen as programmed by nature. In either case science delivers us a human being who has lost the opportunity to choose, grow, change, and decide. David Wheeler's chapter on post-modernism presents the challenge to find a language of faith when shared values have vanished. The scientific challenge now and in the future presents us with debate over whether human beings have any choices at all.

These arguments about science may seem abstract and far-fetched, but the role of science in extending our lives is neither. How long do you expect to live? Most of us will probably give a number under 100 years. The 21st century has invited us to think about doubling that to 200. Most of us have heard something of the cloning debate since the advent of Dolly the sheep. British scientists, with less fanfare, have created headless tadpoles, leading to speculation about when headless people might be created to provide a fresh supply of hearts, kidneys, lungs, and other organs for transplant. If that approach is adopted, many of us can expect to live much longer. Another approach, less controversial, involves overcoming the Hayflick limit. Dr. Leonard Hayflick discovered in 1965 that normal human cells, in a cultured test tube, would divide 50 times and then die of old age. In humans the aging process is linked to the depletion of telomeres when cells divide. If we think of these telomeres as the plastic ends of a shoelace (easier to picture than a chromosome), imagine that each time a cell divides, part of the plastic end is depleted. Eventually the plastic (the telomeres) is gone. Cells can no longer divide.

But what if you have something to keep the plastic end of the shoelace from depleting? Scientists have that now—a gene called telomerase. In scientific experiments the telomeres have been restored to youthful length, and cells began dividing again. Where will this end? Will the 21st century bring us the fountain of youth? In other genetic experiments with the laboratory roundworm, life span was increased to a human equivalent of 340 years. Imagine meeting someone born in 1660! Clearly there is good news in genetic research for many people. Imagine new skin for burn victims. Think about replacing blood vessels or linings for arteries that have hardened.

Science will also bring tremendous challenges to people of faith. What it means to be a human being in the image of God will take on a new dimension. How long a person lives on a crowded planet creates new questions for Christian ethics. How far should we allow ourselves to go in genetic engineering will not be easily decided. The peace treaty between science and faith may not hold as we move into the 21st century. The issues are now very complex, and both science and faith have strong claims about the proper role and place of human beings on our shrinking planet.

(3) *Social and economic changes will drastically alter the way we live in the 21st century.* I graduated from high school in 1960, which means that I grew up in the post-war economic boom years. With post-war Europe in ruins and most of the remainder of the world underdeveloped, America was without serious competitors. It was a good time for many Americans—like my father who came home from the war and went to work.

My father finished his high school diploma when he returned from military duty, and then he tried college for a semester on the G.I. Bill. With two young children to feed and good jobs available, he packed up and went back home. For the next several years my father worked in the local glass factory, and my mother left her war-time job at the telephone company. With very little help from others, my father built a small Cape Cod house. We moved from a four-room cottage behind my grandparents to our new home. The mortgage on that Cape Cod was $85.00 a month.

One never becomes rich as a factory worker, but we had all we really needed. Eventually there were three children, and my mother went back to work—not because of financial need so much as the desire to have a life outside the home. So with my father working in a glass factory and my mother working as a telephone operator, it seemed as if we had enough. A brand new Oldsmobile sat in our driveway. Like the rich person in the parable, we "feasted sumptuously every day" (Luke 16:19). We had clothes, food, cars, shelter, and all the basics. And unless my memory fails me terribly, the cost of goods and services in the 50s was extremely modest. To test my memory, I pulled down an old high school yearbook into which I had tucked a newspaper from November 12, 1959. Here are some of the prices:

- Boneless pork roast (49¢/lb.)
- Cream pies (69¢ ea.)
- Red potatoes (10 lbs./39¢)
- Vacuum cleaner ($20.00)
- Beer ($2.69/case of 24)
- Cotton dresses ($5.88 ea.)

It was about this time that I purchased my first car at a cost of $90.00. It was not a great car, but it ran for two years before I sold it. An adequate used car could be obtained for $200 or $300. Where we lived, the price of gasoline never went above 19 cents a gallon during those years. Our family doctor charged $2.00 a visit, including the penicillin shot that he thought cured everything. Thus, with a family income of about $10,000 from two working adults, all the basic economic needs of our family were easily obtained.

When I go home now, I see a vacant field where the glass factory once gave union jobs to 5,000 men. The telephone office, closed also, no longer offers jobs to high school dropouts like my mother. Certainly the world has changed, but greater shocks lie ahead.

Of course, one major change is the two-income family. The second income is not optional in most families. The reason is clear: real incomes have been falling for American workers who hold nonsupervisory jobs, and those wages will be back to 1950s levels by the time we move the calendar to the year 2000. Typically, people survive falling real incomes by adding another paycheck. In our most recent decades of increased wealth, not all of us have benefited. If you are a baseball player or a skilled professional, your wealth has probably increased lately. The top 20% incomes among us reaped 80% of the new wealth. The vast majority of workers saw the pie get smaller and smaller. And the largest poverty group in America has become children under 18 years of age.

In my 20th-century growing-up experience, jobs were available partly because competition was minimal. My parents, with no education, having survived the Great Depression and a world war, enjoyed rising prosperity and adequate retirement programs, including Social Security. My daughter, who graduated from college with honors and earned a graduate degree, lives in a two-room apartment and must add part-time work on weekends to make ends meet on a teacher's salary in rural Missouri. She is not alone. A full third of all men between the ages of 25 and 35 lack the earning power necessary to keep a family of four above the poverty line.

Recently the news broke that a famous brand shoe manufacturer in Maine was closing production and moving abroad. Several hundred people were put out of work. How many times have we heard the story now? Somewhere beyond our shores, a worker is making a product that will be sold in the U.S. He works every day of the month except for two days off. He works eleven hours a day and is paid about 11 cents an hour. My parents did not have to compete for that job—but my children have to.

And what of my grandson who starts school in the year 2000? If current economic and social trends continue into the 21st century, Jack's world will be as different from today as my 50s world was to my 19th-century grand-parents who rode the horse and buggy. Just as the dinosaurs did not go extinct the day a comet hit the earth and set in motion volcanoes and sulfuric dust, we will not experience overnight transformations. But neither will we be able to stop the effect of the volcanoes erupting around us.

Clearly, there will be less in the 21st century. For those who are highly skilled and highly educated, economic benefits will continue to be there. But good jobs are fading fast now, and there will be many losers—many. America will have a large third world population and a smaller first world population, somewhat comparable to India today. About 1/3 of India lives in the stone age. About 1/3 lives in the 19th century. And the top 1/3 is comprised of the educated elite, the engineers, and professional class. Great cleavages loom ahead for us. Good jobs are moving away. Workers are moving in. For example, large numbers are immigrating north from Mexico. One estimate is that 25,000 undocumented individuals come just into San Diego County each month. If it is true that every child requires $250,000 to properly educate, feed, house, and equip for the day when she will become able to support herself, where will the money come from?

In all probability, it will not come at all in the 21st century for many. The result will be large numbers of uneducated, unemployed, and unhappy people. The possibilities for social disruption are great. There are not enough jails now to contain the crime being bred. Is the answer just more prison space?

The temptation of the affluent will be to retreat. Some may retreat into private communities where gates and guards protect life and property. Home schooling and private academies will proliferate. Even today in communities where public education is strong, private schools are being established. Just recently in Columbia, Missouri, a city that boasts of excellent schools, a new private academy was formed. The retreat into sects, tribes, and fundamentalist groups is likely to grow exponentially. What would happen if the prediction comes true that every grain farmer is going to go broke from Kansas City to Denver going west and from Texas to North Dakota going north? We stopped making shoes in the 20th century. It is quite possible that we will stop growing wheat in the 21st century. After all, if corporate manufacturing moved away, is there reason to believe that corporate farming would not follow were the incentives there?

The potential exists for extremism and fundamentalism to flourish. Blame, rage, and a rhetoric of disrespect have been planted and most surely will bear its ugly fruit in the 21st century. The century ahead is surely a period of extreme uncertainty. But uncertainty is too great a burden for many to bear. The voices of hate will not lack for a following. For many who are left out, there is nothing to lose. There is a great deal of pain to come.

After a recent board meeting at our seminary, most of the time having been spent trying to envision new fund-raising methods for our growing enrollment and being unable to apprehend any definite solutions, a veteran board member and seasoned minister remarked to me: "I've seen things much worse here. Hang in there." As we attempt to envision what our lives and our churches will look like in the 21st century, it would be terrible if we fell into despair because so much of what we want and feel entitled to will be absent. There have been other centuries of uncertainty and struggle. God calls us to be faithful. God's intentions to bless the creation will not diminish, and God's promises to be with us to the end will not be withdrawn.

"Rejoice always, pray without ceasing, give thanks in all circumstances" (1 Thess 5:16-17). I'm certain Paul did not write that from a position of power or privilege. His missionary work was just beginning, and the Christian movement was embryonic. The first century for the church was one of slavery, poverty and extreme inequality. Life was brutally hard. But Paul's confidence in the power of the gospel was greater than his despair over the plight of the world.

Given major denominational changes, given imploding technological/scientific developments, given social and economic upheaval, the 21st century may prove to be as difficult as the 1st century. How will the church respond? How should the church respond? And, forewarned, will we seek to shape rather than just respond to these changes?

In the following chapters, several of our Central Seminary faculty members isolate ideas and issues from their specific fields of expertise in order to sharpen our tools for the challenges ahead. Taken together, these chapters are our attempt to point forward. At the same time, these chapters are our attempt to celebrate the Christ who meets us in the power of the resurrection at every moment, in any and every century.

NOTES

[1]Peter F. Drucker, "The Age of Social Transformation," *The Atlantic Monthly*, November 1994, 53.

[2]Ibid., 54.

BEING THERE
IN THE COMMUNITY OF FAITH
BEYOND BARNA AND EGONOMICS: A PROLOGUE

James Hines

ALL ADULTS TEND NOT TO BE HAPPY, watch too much television, and have little concern for the environment and the well-being of others. Many people reading the interpreters of today's pop culture are buying into such generalizations. They seem to make little allowance for individual differences and appear determined to represent all adults as being of like mind and attitudes.

Although the "Barna Craze" and "Megatrend" prophesies have created an appetite for hearing about culture and societal concerns, they have moved their readers very close to oversimplifying and generalizing very complex human issues. In fact, it appears that much of the energy around interpreting the church and the Christian life is focused on such institutional concerns as worship styles, church ministry environments, and changing church leadership patterns while often ignoring the challenges related to individual value systems and commitment to personal growth. I realize that by adding my insights I may add to the confusion and feeding frenzy. I believe, however, that too much of the achieved status of adults is found in contributing to institutional systems. Subsequently, adults do not wish to experience church as a place where they habitually base their personal identity upon institutional usefulness or broad generalizations about their commitments.

This anti-institutionalism goes beyond "egonomics"[1] and the failure of institutions to customize desires and/or services or making appeals to their individuality. Read in any popular trend book today, and you find out what adults born between 1945 and 1955 have known for a long time: This adult cohort group of ten years consistently challenges traditional governmental, societal, cultural, and religious norms. These adults (a group I prefer to call the "true" baby boom generation and/or the "transitional generation") find it humorous that the rest of the adult population are continually surprised at their population size, economic influence, and resistance to governmental, cultural, social, and religious norms.

This transitional cohort group continually bridges the gap between attitudes and values of those born before 1945 and those born after 1955. It is this generation of middle-aged adults who are now theoretically positioned to lead in governmental, social, cultural, and religious experiences, and that scares the daylights out of many informed persons. After all, it was this generation that experienced the full impact of Vietnam, race riots, national assassinations, runaway national inflation, declining job markets, the greening effects, Sputnik, and the expansion of the Christian church as both a denomination and a local church institution.

The responses of this transitional generation to these major events were quite different from those of the generation that came before them. For the most part, they did not display a national movement toward making personal sacrifices for "the American Way" and thus running out and signing up to go to war. Many in this transitional generation became conscientious objectors and/or fled to Canada or parts unknown, publicly burned the American flag, and staged sit-ins in government and university administration buildings. They publicly challenged traditional institutional values, made broad allowances for the expression of human sexuality, and became principal players in establishing today's drug culture. Yet, this generation appeared to be marked by stark contradiction. It also exhibited strong value placements related to involvement in national election campaigns, protecting the global environment, working to affirm racial equality, and supporting national two-year volunteer service organizations such as the Peace Corps and denominational mission programs.

Simultaneously, many in this cohort group looked at the church and questioned traditional religious values and practices. Given America's growing globalization, many in this transitional group saw the church lacking in any serious value for humankind. Many were rebuffed by the "just get 'em saved" syndrome, a syndrome perceived as being removed from genuine compassion, respect for the person, and regard for human dignity. The church as community appeared to lack the respect for individual differences related to major issues such as race and gender acceptance, and exhibited little tolerance for lesser issues such as dress, hair styles and length, and beards.

At a time when the church should have been expressing significant outrage related to war and famine, it was perceived as practicing church growth methods that used popular telemarketing campaigns such as "Jesus Is the Real Thing" and "I Found It." Such growth practices became church and denominational trends that appeared to help the institutional church grow in members, buildings, and budgets. These secular practices seemed to reinforce the belief that the church was becoming a self-serving, egocentric organization that reflected the values of a religious middle class social club where dues were nominal and control was everything.

This transitional generation has been required to adjust to the new high-tech culture of the cohort groups that followed them. The ethos of this high-tech culture consists of voice-activated word processing, portable cellular phones, CDs, and the Concorde airplane. This transitional cohort group has been required to make major life adjustments related to the transformation of our Western culture from low-tech to high-tech, sometimes forgetting that just a few years ago high-tech meant Smith/Corona cartridge typewriters, rotary dial phones, 8-track players, and the DC-10 airplane. This new, high-tech culture is very different from the more melancholy era of peace marches, coffeehouses, and Woodstock. The very ethos of this new era has created an environment that has redefined community as something you experience as you have lively discussions in a "chat room" while drinking a cup of cappuccino.

Current publications and discussions give evidence that the developing attitudes and fears of the younger generations are driving wedges between the various adult cohort groups where the newly emerging elderly, that "baby boomer" group, are seen as the enemy. This enemy sponges off the federal government and takes jobs away from youth, thereby robbing the next several generations of their future. This enemy is generally considered far too liberal about social activism, is entirely too accepting of diversity, is too anti-institution, and is too prone to inclusiveness, in graphic contrast to the conservative tendencies of both their older and younger age group counterparts. Such a schizophrenic enemy shows a conforming mentality that values belonging to a group in which common interests and/or characteristics are shared and also a liberating mentality where individual differences and freedom of personal expression are valued.

The impacts of these obvious age group differences are extensive and may very well be foundational for understanding the plight of religious faith and practice. In fact, our seeming inability to transcend our own emerging intergenerational culture may very well account for the increasing tensions between clergy and parishioners related to understanding the local church, individual personal growth, and Christian activism.

Introduction

Having been in Christian ministry for twenty-five years and a "conservative transitional adult," my family and I have always been at church. My wife and I required our children to attend both Sunday School and worship, allowing them to choose all other activities. When they became teenagers, we told them that when they finished high school we would no longer require them to attend Sunday School and worship. We based such a decision upon the belief that they must take ownership of their own Christian journey. Our obvious prayer was they would choose to attend based upon their own Christian values and beliefs related to the importance of the church and their need for Christian fellowship. One can imagine my surprise when my oldest daughter chose not to attend Sunday School or worship. In fact, she announced to her mother and me that she was quitting church altogether. She expressed to us a strong belief in Christ but asserted, "Dad, why do I want to attend church when my non-Christian friends treat and accept me better than Christians at church?"

At first I sought to help her reflect on the theological reasons for attending church activities, stressing the importance of individual responsibility in making the church a good place to attend. I may have even said something rather dumb like, "We are only as big as the hypocrites we hide behind." Since her pronouncement of "I quit," however, we have had many excellent conversations related to the kingdom of God and the church.

Our conversations have caused me, once again, to raise the question as to why many "longtime Christians" who ought to be teachers, are still learners needing someone to teach them again the basic elements of God's word?[2] My personal response to this question rests in the belief that many Christians have failed to take ownership of their faith, neglecting the integration of faith into their life journey. Many Christians can describe every minute detail related to their conversion experience, but struggle with understanding God in their personal experience. In fact, not only do Christians struggle with sensing God in their personal relationships, they, more often than not, cling to a self-sufficiency, withdraw to their homes, and live in isolation, often ignoring the fact that they are bound together with both God and others.

Another response to this question relates to how Baptists view baptism. We understand, with Payne and Brewer, that "baptism by water is an important rite of passage which marks the beginning of a lifelong pilgrimage (conversion)."[3] Baptists have even come to realize that baptism is a sign that puts us in touch with the story of the universe and recalls the original saving event of God's work for us and our incorporation into the community of faith (salvation). Likewise, Baptists have historically accepted baptism as a symbolic act that marks the beginning of one's life journey of faith (sanctification) that ideally carries us through life to death. Such a conversionistic theology challenges persons to become Christ's disciples, living in the midst of a world that may or may not always understand what it means "to follow," a journey that implies growth both spiritually and personally.[4]

However, I fear that somewhere along the way we as Baptists are losing our moorings. Somewhat like my teenage daughter, some Christians are saying, "I quit," abandoning the church, and neglecting their own spiritual growth. Other Christians are staying active in the church, but, for all practical purposes, have lost the holy intent for which they gather. Yet, the church is not without hope, as Christians do not have to engage in spiritual bumper cars. We can replace meaningless activity with empowering spiritual growth and find renewal in coming together as a spiritual faith community.

CHURCH: INSTITUTION VERSUS COMMUNITY OF FAITH

Talk with pastors today, and they will quickly tell you, in some way, how the church as an institution shapes much of their time and energy. Talk with a pastor long enough in an honest, private environment, and stories will surface that would give counselors nightmares. These stories reflect personal experiences related to conflicts of interests, unresolved church membership controversies, and ambiguous jurisdictions related to pastor and committee responsibilities versus member expectations. Added to these interpersonal conflict issues, or perhaps as an outgrowth of them, the church appears to many outsiders as a nonprofit institution that has turned itself inward, a tax-exempt nonprofit agency that engages in business for the primary purpose and benefit of its financial contributors and involved membership.

These church stories tell of interdenominational and interchurch competition, protectivism, and selective caring. These stories of competition relate to higher and higher attendance figures, bigger budgets, more staff, better buildings, and more creative programs. This competition is stirred by success stories of the church across town or what some other denomination is doing that is working! A natural outgrowth of this highly charged, competitive church and denominational environment is membership protectivism, a protectivism that too often sees its primary role as a watchguard of the church. After all, now that buildings are built and programs and staff are in place, they must be maintained and preferably improved.

This protectivism surfaces in not just wanting new members, but ultimately the right members, members who are not from Samaria, in other words, "those persons" who are outcast and/or of a different ethnic background.

A pastor friend told me a story related to his efforts to establish a child-care program in a small rural Texas church. He had done his homework and covered all his bases, and the church seemed enthusiastic and ready to approve the program. The Wednesday evening the program was to be discussed and approved went well until an older woman stood up and said, "Brother Jake, I just thought of one question that has not been asked. Will there be any brown babies (meaning Hispanic babies) in this day care?" My friend replied, "Well, I hope so" (thus indicating an openness to reaching the Hispanic community). Jake said that little else was discussed as the program proposal was defeated.

The poor tend to be a potential drain since they cannot give much, yet come with great need; besides, they prefer their own church and people. What surfaces is a form of selective caring, caring that is primarily internalized. In fact, look at the average church budget and see what percentage is spent internally versus what percentage goes beyond the walls of the church.

This selective caring is not just limited to those outside the church. Look how we care for some of our own. I have observed numerous churches raise large amounts of money for some members who had major medical expenses, while not even visiting and helping others. We, at times unknowingly, will go out of our way for weddings, funerals, and special events for some in the church, while barely tipping our hat to others. Over time, the increased value placement upon competition, protectivism, and selective caring has caused many Christians to lose a type of church synergy in which freedom and responsibility are disregarded and the prophetic voice ignored. In fact, I fear that many Christians are in danger of developing a type of "Christian narcissism,"[5] which removes them from the cutting edge of society and feeds their own spiritual and material hungers.

The influence of Christian narcissism upon the institutional church has an emotional and spiritual drain upon the average Christian, negatively influencing discretionary time given to the church. It has so shaped and reshaped membership understanding of what it means to be and do church that Christians are in danger of losing any real sense of a moral social order founded upon the deep roots of profound Christian beliefs. To this narcissistic perspective, we must add the barrage of negative information received from modern technology.

As a child growing up in the 1950s, I remember hearing about the devastating impact of war and famine. However, today my children and I see starvation and killings while they are actually occurring! One would think that such visual reminders would create a strong personal and national outcry. Instead, we have become a people and a nation that has grown accustomed to hearing and seeing tragedies, so that we tend to view such events through the lens of indifference. After all, the poor and hurting we will always have with us. Subsequently, one need not wonder why many Christians have difficulty grasping a greater global awareness and are numb and complacent towards suffering and death in the world.

What we must do is develop the ability and disposition to participate in the church, the community of faith. Today, most of us live separated from neighbors we do not know. When we are sick or dying, we are tended by strangers. And too often, our birthdays and anniversaries pass uncelebrated. Subsequently, too often our churches are places too anonymous to satisfy our need for belonging and recognition. Therefore, we need a community of faith where cooperation, celebration, and caring are benchmarks; where relationships take risks related to mutual openness; where individuals gather with friends and family to talk about what is important; feasting, laughing, and weeping together.[6]

We must also develop an appreciation for the meaning and importance of being a community of faith, recognizing that the organized church has changed radically in the past century. But that does not mean that Christians can escape their responsibility to the church as a community of faith; rather, we must be willing to learn from each other, choosing to collectively create new expressions of ministry, resourcing, and support. It is a delusion to think that Christians can say and do nothing about their religious beliefs, live removed from a community of faith, and still have a strong moral and religious influence upon society. The Christian faith has a powerful influence upon the direction of society. If this influence is to be positive, growing Christians must have an interpretation of life founded upon Scripture, interpreted in the context of a broadening global awareness. This interpretation of life must be an effective guide to all experiences, addressing ethical and spiritual vacuums.

Today's church cannot escape the responsibility for making the gospel relevant to persons in their human situation. In doing this, we must know people as they are. In reality, we must seek to empathize with or at least have sympathetic understanding for what it means to be a youth, an eccentric, a deviate, a middle-of-the-roader, or a social outcast.

For indeed, Jesus was concerned about all persons and all of each person: body, mind, spirit, environment, future, ideas, relationships, burdens, handicaps, sins, struggles, and sufferings. You see, the Lord first sought to lead a person to God and then to lead in paths of righteousness. In essence, if the church is God's plan for redeeming lost persons, then it must speak to persons as they are and where they are, regardless of who they are. The real starting point will always be with each of us taking ownership of our faith and seeing this ownership as an integral aspect of life's journey, a journey that presupposes ownership of one's personal growth.

PERSONAL GROWTH: OWNERSHIP VERSUS DISPLACEMENT

I am convinced that one of the greatest imperatives of the Christian faith community is to promote growth: growth that provides a climate for the full sanctification process to take place; growth that gradually transforms persons into the image and likeness of Jesus Christ; growth that is evidenced by hope, peace, and joy. In fact, I fear that many Christians have failed to realize the importance of growth in grace and Christian character, adopting an attitude of contentment within an ordinary Christian lifestyle that stifles new growth.[7]

Part of this apathetic contentment rests with Christians failing to take ownership of their own spiritual development and allowing their ethical and spiritual lives to be primarily private affairs of the heart. Christians have been content with personal growth that comes primarily from what they hear from the pulpit or in a Sunday School class. Many Christians, and I fear Baptists in particular, have failed to exercise what E. Y. Mullins called their right to exercise private judgment in interpreting the Scripture. By yielding their soul competency[8] over to a preacher or teacher, Christians fall prey to a narrow-mindedness that seeks to coerce others in matters of religion, thereby supporting a "gospel of tyranny." Such a gospel fosters blind and arrogant fellowship to pseudo-creeds, suggesting a narrow form of piety that discounts the varied colorations of true Christian piety.

Our ethical and spiritual lives cannot be based simply, as Paul Wilkes stated, on a "feel good experience . . . [that ignores] both pain and joy in our spiritual [and ethical] experiences."[9] Rather, it must be based upon a genuine coming together on the part of the faith community, a coming together of community where dialogue is preferred over monologue, where critical and spiritual thinking is endorsed over creedal conformity, where love is chosen over hate, where humility is embraced over arrogance, and where hope is adopted over despair.

At the core of this imperative of personal ownership is the enhancement of relationships with both God and humankind. These relationships must be based upon acceptance, active listening, and encouragement blended with accountability. One's growth with both God and others demands honesty in relationships that genuinely and caringly address needs related to security, recognition, and meaningful interactions. The community of faith must not base its relationships upon distorted images of others, such as senile, unskilled, liberal, or fundamentalist. We must claim what it means to be a community of faith, realizing that at its very root community means having more concern for the "affairs of the heart" than "business affairs."

For growth to take place at all, the church must foster a consciousness of God as a reality in our human experience, a sense of personal relationship with God, where we are open to what God is doing with the whole of our life experiences.[10] Nothing is without its meaning. A misfortune or celebration may do more to give us understanding of the deeper levels of human experience than years of knowledge-based information about God. We must also develop an understanding and appreciation of the personality, life, and teachings of Jesus that will encourage commitment to him and his cause, and manifest itself in life experiences and conduct. Harvie Branscomb asserts that it is "in his own character and in his insights into the realm of spiritual values Jesus reveals to us the character of God and God's purpose for our lives." Like Jesus, we must confront life issues and decide them on the basis of courage and faith and not by foreknowledge.

Jesus taught that love must be the central and dominant element in the personal growth of those who would do the will of God. First Corinthians 13 addresses the character by which we all are to live; we are to live first and foremost by love, but not just any love. We are to live by a love that is self-giving and forgiving, a love that is redemptive. Church members struggle with how to express collective love and redemption.

A deacon friend of mine told me about how his pastor of many years was going to be indicted on charges of indecent exposure. As it became evident to the church that the charges had substance, the deacon body asked the church to remove the pastor from leadership of the church, but not without paying for counseling and providing financially for him and his family. The vote surfaced during a Wednesday evening with the highest Wednesday evening attendance the church had ever experienced. The proposal passed by a very narrow margin. It seems the church struggled with whether to express the nurture of redemptive love or the wrath of redemptive love.

The decision as to what to do with the pastor was not the real issue for the church. The church's real struggle was with the membership's ability and disposition to participate in and contribute constructively to a redemptive community. It appears that, like many churches, my friend's church was struggling with how to "do church," rather than fostering a progressive and continuous development of "being" Christlike, where self-giving and forgiving characteristics are marked by humility, sincerity, and faith.

ACTIVISM: DOING VERSUS BEING

Less the clergy, or anyone else, be too hard on Christians in the church, one would do well to remember they are where they have been led. Since 1952, Baptist ministers have been schooled by seminaries and supported by publishing houses to administer the church. This training involved important issues related to church administration, educational planning, and leadership training. It wisely focused upon key concepts such as administering church educational organizations, leadership personnel (paid and volunteer), training teachers and leaders to teach and lead, and administering educational support services. Two key books promoting such educational administration and church leadership training in Southern Baptist life were *Christian Education Handbook*, edited by Bruce P. Powers, and *Educational Ministry of a Church*, edited by Charles A. Tidwell. These two friends and colleagues and their peers[11] were key influences in shaping a healthy understanding as to how to do the work of the church.

Likewise, many adults in the church who are now forty and older experienced high quality training through religious conference centers and various local, state, and national training workshops. Like their church staff counterparts, they were trained and challenged through workshops to develop organizational skills related to deacon ministries, Sunday school ministries, church growth strategies, evangelism, missions education, and discipleship. All this preparation and training created a large cohort group of adults who understood/stand how to "do church." They were trained in what it meant to give of themselves and their time to the life of the church, while being encouraged through preaching and Bible study to growing spiritually.

Yet, somewhere between the educational training and preaching and teaching of the Bible, many persons, identified with mainline denominations, lost and/or failed to discover what it means to "be" the church. It appears that somewhere along the way the people of God patterned their activism in the church after Western capitalism, thereby allowing the focus of the church to be more aligned with issues of production and success rather than personal spiritual growth.

This concept touched me personally when I accepted my first church staff position. My family and I had a wonderful call experience with both church members and staff. The time with committee members and staff was rich in prayer, dialogue, and worship. The Sunday I went in "view of a call" included a powerful time of worship and personal connection. By the afternoon, there was a clear sense of call to the church, and I was looking forward to the last event of the day, the church membership reception. Early during the reception, however, a businessman approached me, introduced himself, and said, "We are looking forward to your coming and know that within the first year you will bring enough people into the church to pay for your salary!" At the time, I shrugged off his comments and did not allow it to deter me from what I knew to be right. I simply allowed his comments to quickly become a faded memory.

My first Sunday at the church rekindled this memory, however. I was walking down a hallway. Coming from the opposite direction, heading full steam ahead in my direction was, for all appearances, a very "classy" older woman. From a stereotypical perspective, she looked almost angelic. Her head was crowned with beautiful white hair that was well groomed. She wore on her face a wonderful smile. Her frame was small, short, and frail but sturdy. She moved within inches from me, stopped me, and asked, "Are you that new minister that started today?" I replied, probably with some pride, "Yes, Ma'am, I am." At that point, she shook her finger in my face and said with great force, "Well, just remember one thing; I pay your salary!" Fortunately, her response was tempered by more positive responses from others.

The problem with addressing the challenge of capitalistic activity upon true Christian living is that most of our energies are not directed towards subjective concepts such as sanctification, the ongoing process of being redeemed, changed to newness of life. We historically focus upon Sunday morning Bible study attendance, budget figures, the number of outreach contacts made, or whether one serves as deacon or teacher. We tend to focus more upon events themselves rather than upon what the individual is to experience. Subsequently, many assume that because individuals do all the right things for the church—attend, lead, and give—their lives must reflect spiritual discipline and practice. Evidently, along the way, in its attempt to train Christian leadership, the church failed to emphasize the "being" attributes that guide Christians in viewing life through a renewed faith commitment. Jürgen Moltmann said it well when he wrote,

> If life is lived in embodiment and if it is committed in its earthly context, it becomes vulnerable and mortal. But because it is spent, it brings fruit. . . . Surrendering one's life means going out of oneself, exposing oneself, committing oneself and loving. In this affirmation life becomes alive in the truly human sense.[12]

The difficulty in measuring subjective attributes such as commitment, hope, joy, peace, or happiness has, in part, caused us to avoid them. After all, can we or are we willing to make a value judgement as to whether one person is more committed, loving, forgiving, or happy than another? Is it even possible to guide someone in areas of growth development such as commitment, joy, peace, and hope? Yes, we can give illustrations as to when someone is happy or joyful or even spiritually mature. But we are uneasy at saying one Christian is "better" at being a joyful Christian than another. Or better still, we, perhaps for good reason, refuse to say this one Christian is more spiritual than another. We prefer to avoid the "being" issues and use the "doing" attributes to illustrate spiritual maturity.

Thus, the fact that adults have been active in the program life of the church does not necessarily mean they have matured spiritually in the faith. Many ministers I talk with tell me people are disengaging from the church. Yet, there is little doubt that religious concerns are becoming more intense among persons of acknowledged faith. What appears to be lacking, however, is appreciation for and development of basic spiritual growth skills related to prayer and meditation, solitude and silence, study and submission, and confession and worship.

Conclusion

Christian faith is not by design the promotion of the strong; rather, it recognizes weakness while accepting the inward truth about self. Our faith calls us not to be a great people, but a deeper people. Our Christian faith calls us to a spiritual life that would move us beyond surface living while inviting us to explore empowering attributes such as meekness, patience, forgiveness, and purity. It calls us to express in all of life true love, joy, peace, and gentleness. We must focus upon the transformation that takes place in human life when

God comes to us in both Word and Spirit. Christians must foster a new consciousness of God as a reality in their human experience, being open to what God is doing in their lives, while discovering new and creative ways to meaningfully participate in the life of the church.

Christians must never forget that faith is more than a verbal expression of belief in God. It is a spiritual discipline and practice that entails relationships, commitments, and an openness to the mysteries of God. Christians must not just talk about faith in God; they must lean upon the very hope of their faith. Such a faith and hope calls one to reach beyond the circumstances of the moment[13] and rely upon the hope experienced in God who called them into being symbolized by their baptism [redemption], who guides in their Christian journey [sanctification], and who will receive them at the end of their journey into the Kingdom [regeneration].[14]

NOTES

[1]Egonomics is used here to mean the epitome of egocentrism where me, myself, and I are the driving forces that shape personal and economic decisions.

[2]Heb 5:12.

[3]Barbara Payne and Earl Brewer, *Gerontology in Theological Education: Local Program Development* (New York: The Haworth Press, 1989) 118.

[4]Ibid.

[5]For further treatment of narcissism, see Christopher Lasch, *The Culture of Narcissism: American Life in an Age of Diminishing Expectations* (New York: Warner Books, 1979) and Warren McWilliams, *Christ and Narcissus: Prayer in a Self-Centered World* (Ontario: Herald Press, 1992).

[6]Sam Keen, *Fire in the Belly* (New York: Bantam Books) 229.

[7]E. Y. Mullins, *Baptist Beliefs* (Philadelphia: Judson Press, 1921) 48, 49.

[8]"Soul competency"—For relationship of this phrase to Southern Baptist beliefs, see, Herschel H. Hobbs, *The Baptist Faith and Message* (Nashville: Convention Press, 1971) 7-12.

[9]Paul Wilkes, "The Hands That Would Shape Our Souls," *The Atlantic Monthly*, December 1990, 84.

[10]J. M. Price, James H. Chapman, L. L. Carpenter, and Yarborough, *A Survey of Religious Education* (New York: Ronald Press Co., 1959) 142, 143.

[11]See *Administering Christian Education* (1964/1989) by Robert K. Bower, *A Ministering Church* (1960) by Gaines S. Dobbins, *The Effective Minister of Education* (1993) by Jerry M. Stubblefield, *Pastoral Leadership* (1986/1990) by Robert D. Dale.

[12]Moltmann, Jürgen, *God in Creation: A New Theology of Creation and the Spirit of God* (San Francisco: Harper & Row, 1985) 269.

[13]Payne and Brewer, 59.

[14]Ibid, 59, 60.

HIGH CHURCH, LOW CHURCH

WHICH WAY IS WORSHIP GOING?

Mike Graves

I WAS BORN INTO A ROMAN CATHOLIC FAMILY, so to speak. Actually, my mother had been raised Nazarene, but my father was Roman Catholic, so to speak. That is, he was not devout. But when my parents married, they agreed to bring up their son in the Catholic tradition. I was christened as an infant in the Saint James Catholic Church in Houston, Texas. I did not attend catechetical school, and for that matter, we did not attend mass regularly. In fact, we stopped going to church altogether by the time I was in the third grade.

Still, I have memories of those Sundays in that massive cathedral. I remember how the light and dark played off each other in mysterious ways. I vividly recall dark cavernous places with statues surrounded by candles. I remember the beautiful stained glass windows that surrounded me. The liturgy told us when to stand, when to sit, and when to kneel. I also remember a priest holding up a chalice and a wafer before us all and mumbling something in Latin. It was all quite beyond me.

The next time I remember being in a worship service was not until the seventh grade, when some kids from the United Pentecostal church down the street invited me to attend with them. There I experienced a different kind of mumbling, another kind of "tongue" that I could not understand. I do not recall the sanctuary having any stained glass windows. There certainly were not any statues of Mary surrounded by candles. What I sensed, however, was a spirit of fervency.

It was not until the end of my first year of college that I went to church again. Only, this time something happened. A young woman had been witnessing to me, and in the spring of 1977, I had a dramatic conversion experience. I became a believer and started attending that church regularly. The worship was simple and traditional. Friendly announcements preceded the singing of familiar hymns and readings from the Psalms. The sermon was the climactic piece, followed by a time for worshipers to make decisions (in private, not public). The church was a nondenominational Bible church, and the pastor made it clear that when it came to types of worship, charismatic styles were demonic.

Such a pronouncement probably would not have bothered me too much if it were not for the fact that I was then engaged to a young woman whose family was from the Assembly of God tradition. Actually, her mom and sisters had grown up Southern Baptist, but had joined the Assembly of God church after my fiancee's father died.

In God's providence, and to keep the peace, my wife and I became Southern Baptists. I served on staff at two Southern Baptist churches before going to Southwestern Baptist Theological Seminary in Fort Worth, Texas. Including the two churches prior to seminary, and the churches we attended or I served as pastor during seminary, we experienced a variety of worship patterns. Some of them were formal, others casual. Some of them were large, some small. One church was what they called "contemporary." In reaction to my "high church" childhood, my preference as a young adult was casual, "low church" worship. In seminary we visited a Baptist church with formal worship only once. That was enough!

Then something happened, something in many ways akin to my conversion experience, only this change related to worship practices. I had graduated with my Ph.D. and was teaching at Midwestern Baptist Theological Seminary in Kansas City, Missouri. Slowly, but surely, I began to want to sing "Joyful, Joyful, We Adore Thee" more than "O How He Loves You and Me." Instead of acoustical guitars, I wanted to hear the pipe organ. Advent and Lent, mere words from my past, suddenly took on significance. My tastes were changing, and I could not figure out why.

During this time, I had become good friends with my colleague Randall Bradley who taught church music and worship. One day we were browsing in the Baptist Book Store on campus when I picked up a copy of Robert Webber's *Evangelicals on the Canterbury Trail.*[1] What I read were stories very much like my own, of people who had grown up in liturgical traditions who, having rejected the formality, were suddenly drawn back to it.

In his poem, "The Dry Salvages," T. S. Eliot wrote: "We had the experience but missed the meaning." Suddenly my childhood experiences that had been beyond me made sense. What I sought was something literally "beyond me," what theologians call the transcendent qualities of God. I wanted my worship of the Lord to contain a sense of the mystery and majesty of God.

THE DIVERSE WORSHIP LANDSCAPE

Almost ten years later I am still reflecting on my own pilgrimage, but now I better understand the current preoccupation with the subject of worship. On any given Sunday in most any city we could expect to find a range of worship options, everything from "Gloria Patri" and robed processions to hand-clapping choruses projected on screens, even snake handling in the name of God in some rural settings. High church, low church: which way is worship going?

Interestingly enough, this diversity can be experienced within the Baptist faith. I have worshiped in Baptist churches where the worship styles resembled everything from Episcopalian to United Pentecostal. Historically, this has been a great strength of Baptist life, autonomy of the local church. Every church is free to believe and practice as it feels led by the Spirit of God.

Unfortunately, the diverse options have resulted in what scholars have labeled the "worship wars." In the churches, ministers and members alike are talking about worship, only not all of the conversations are civil. Some congregations bicker over styles of worship. These worship wars concern squabbles over what kinds of music are legitimate in worship, whether prayers should be spontaneous or prepared, whether to have a time where people greet one another during the service, and serious discussions over the appropriateness of applause in worship. I find it parabolic in a way that scholars in the field cannot even agree on whether to spell the word "worshipping" with two p's, or "worshiping" with only one p. I have seen it both ways.

Ironically, in recent years the more formal traditions have begun to experiment with freer forms of praise, while charismatic congregations have embraced liturgical renewal.[2] One wonders how these groups will view their former preferences once they finish crossing over.

Historically, Baptists have embraced two diverse worship styles—the Charleston tradition and the Sandy Creek tradition. These traditions predate the formation of the Baptist denominations, but they still reflect preferences among different Baptists today.[3]

The Charleston tradition originated with the congregation of the First Baptist Church of Charleston, South Carolina, which was the first Baptist church in the southern part of the United States. Begun in 1695, its worship exhibited order, reverence, and a roughly equal emphasis on the sermon and the Lord's Supper. Worshipers in this tradition were typically well educated and cultured.

The Sandy Creek tradition arose out of the Great Awakenings in the 1750s. Its worship exhibited fervor, emotionalism, and a roughly equal emphasis on the sermon and invitation, instead of the Supper. Worshipers in this tradition were a part of the frontier spirit in America's move westward. In addition, they were typically suspicious of education.

Until fairly recently, the worship landscape in Baptist life consisted of these two traditions with some mild blending. Classifying the myriad of approaches to worship today is much more complicated. One scholar, Lloyd Mims, has categorized five approaches: liturgical, traditional, blended, contemporary/informal, and seeker sensitive. The differences occur in relation to types of songs, kinds of musical instruments, styles of ministerial leadership in the service, the presence or lack of responsive readings, styles of public prayer, and even preaching styles. In some senses, the differences can even be sensed in the mood of the service, a somewhat indescribable feel within the worship service.

So which way is worship going in our culture? Obviously, the popular trend is toward more contemporary approaches to worship. Still, there are many who abhor such trends. What the church needs, however, is not a definitive taxonomy of worship types from which the churches might pick and choose the way Sunday Schools select literature. Something else is needed altogether, and that something is reformation.

REFORM, NOT FORM

Worship discussions often fail to note the kinds of questions being asked these days. Most are "how" questions, issues related to methodology and utility. "How can we make our worship services more vital?" "How can we get the younger generation more interested?" "How can we teach our people to praise God?" "How can we attract worshipers of different generations within the same service?" These are vital questions, no doubt, but they are secondary to another set of issues—"what" questions.

"What" questions ask such things as: "What does it mean to worship God?" "What happens when we worship?" "What does our worship say about God, ourselves, and our world?" "What does it mean to be the church at worship in a culture that appears to be moving away from God?" A preoccupation with forms of worship will not lead to authentic and lasting renewal. Reformation is more than reforming. Reformation in worship must delve into the heart of worship, the theological nature of worship. For that to happen, two things are needed: (1) a clear grasp of the purpose of worship and (2) an evaluation of worship theologically. Let us consider both, beginning with the purpose of worship.

THE PURPOSE OF WORSHIP

Martin Marty has said, "Worship is pointless, but significant."[4] The significant part is obvious enough. It is the "pointless" part that wakes us up. The phrase bothers us, of course, because our culture has ingrained within us an appreciation for doing over being.

In America, most people define themselves by means of their occupation. On an airplane, the person seated next to us asks, "So what do you do for a living?" "Why, I'm a professor at a Baptist seminary. What do you do for a living?" These phrases are so commonplace, we no longer flinch at them. But notice how doing and living are confused. "What do I *do* for a *living*? I eat and drink and breathe. I think and reflect. I interact with the people in my life." Of course, I would not recommend giving such an answer to a complete stranger, but it is worth noting how we rarely think of ourselves as human beings. Human doing is more like it.

This has profound consequences for how we approach worship. For one thing, we project this sense of doing onto God. What a tragedy! Most worshipers are incapable of distinguishing the difference between God's character of being and God's actions. For example, the act of praise entails ascribing worth to God in relation to who God is. In contrast, thanksgiving means expressing gratitude for what God has done. Ask most worshipers to praise God, however, and one will most likely hear statements related to God's actions, not God's character. Thanksgiving says, "I thank you, O Lord, for the forgiveness of sins through Jesus Christ." Praise declares, "I praise you, O Lord, for you alone are holy." Unable to distinguish being from doing, worship becomes a matter of utilitarian interest: "What have you done for me lately, God?"

The second thing that happens when doing and being are confused relates to the worshiper's own identity. Unfortunately, in our culture, worship has become a form of spiritual therapy. The biblical concept of worship in both testaments is that of offering to God. It is a relatively modern notion that allows worshipers to complain, "I just don't get anything out of that kind of worship."

Consider a parable: A couple is running behind schedule, hurriedly getting dressed so as not to be late. In the car they discuss the usual things— work, kids, and projects needing attention around the house. Finally they arrive. They pull into the parking lot and fight for a space not too far away. Someone greets them at the door with a warm smile and a handshake. In addition, they are handed the usual printed materials. Once inside, she says she needs to use the restroom. He waits patiently in the foyer, smiling politely at the people he sees. Seated, they make casual conversation with those around them—sporting news and the weather are common topics. Everyone begins to quiet down as it is time to begin. The conductor appears, and the symphony is underway.

The parable causes us to ask, What happens in worship that is different from being entertained? What does the church gathered for worship offer that no other enterprise on earth can match? If worship is offering to God, rather than complaining about what we get out of worship, we should examine what we are putting into such services.

The concept of participating in worship is a foreign notion to many worshipers. It is not uncommon to hear church members speak of the chancel area as stage and the congregation as audience. Søren Kierkegaard, a Danish philosopher and theologian, offered his own parable about worship. Using the analogy of the theater, Kierkegaard noted how we traditionally view the production of worship: the congregation is the audience, the players are the ministers who are paid to perform, and God is the prompter who whispers lines for the ministers to utter. What a totally inadequate view of worship, noted Kierkegaard. True worship is not passive, but active. The members of the congregation are the players, acting out the divine drama. The ministers are the prompters, helping the players to know their lines. As for the audience, it is God who takes it all in.[5]

As Welton Gaddy notes, "Worship is for God. Only!"[6] The German word for worship captures this idea wonderfully. *Gottesdienst* is frequently translated as "divine service," but that does not begin to do justice to the subtleties of the word. It takes a lengthy English phrase to capture the gist of its meaning. *Gottesdienst* is the service God has rendered to us, which we in return render to God. Worship truly is for God, first and foremost. It is done for God, in response to who God is and what God has done.

There is an English word that also conveys some wonderful truths about worship, a term frequently heard, yet frequently misunderstood. "Liturgy" often refers to "high church" styles of worship. The term comes from the Greek (Acts 13:2), meaning "the work of the people." All worship, however, no matter its style, is to be the work of the people, everything from leading the congregation in reciting the Apostles' Creed to performing a liturgical dance. Each person has a gift to offer in worship (1 Cor 14:26).

Evaluating Worship Theologically

Properly understood, an evaluation of worship should not be based on what worshipers like or dislike, but what God prefers. As such, we must evaluate worship theologically in a myriad of categories. Here we will examine briefly three of the more important categories: the nature of God, the nature of humanity, and the nature of the church. Within each, delicate balances must be considered.

The Nature of God

The first balance relates to what theologians call the tension between God's transcendence and imminence. Transcendence refers to God as removed and supreme, while imminence relates to God's nearness and intimate nature. Both are scriptural truths. Both are worship truths. Unfortunately, one usually wins out over the other.

The architecture of the place of worship, the language, the very mood of the service—all these things evidence whether transcendence or imminence is being emphasized, especially the music. The appropriate question for reformation of worship, therefore, is not: "Should we sing classical hymns or the newer choruses?" Certain tunes and texts convey the nearness and intimacy of God, while others remind us of God's removed and supreme otherness. Both should be present in worship! In some "high church" services worshipers rarely sense the warm presence of God, whereas in some "low church" or contemporary approaches worshipers rarely sense the awesome majesty and mystery of God. Worshipers need both!

The second balance relates to God's faithfulness (or predictability) on the one hand and God's freedom on the other. In terms of worship, the issue is maintaining a balance between order and spontaneity. The structure (or lack of it) in our worship services says something about our view of God. We try in vain to box up the Almighty.

Israel's own history reminds us that God never desired a temple over a tabernacle. God wished to move freely among the children of Israel. After the Israelites' deportation to Babylon, they wondered how worship would be possible. The answer, of course, was the synagogue, a precursor to the New Testament church. Israel's history vividly reminds us that while God will not be boxed, God will always be present where the faithful gather in worship.

Carol Doran and Thomas Troeger note that true worship typically happens between the extremes of spontaneity and structure.[7] Unfortunately, so-called "high church" traditions lean toward order at the expense of spontaneity, while more contemporary approaches try to avoid predictability at all costs. Of course, even the most free-flowing charismatic styles of worship often have a routine order of worship. It is just not always printed. As for the more structured services of worship, leaders would do well to recall what Jesus said about the Spirit of God: "The wind blows where it chooses" (John 3:8). As a friend of mine, who is a United Methodist minister, puts it, he thinks his denomination's slogan ought to be changed from "Catch the Spirit" to, "If you're lucky, the Spirit might catch you!" Good point!

C. S. Lewis offered a wonderful analogy when it comes to structure and familiarity in worship. You are only dancing, noted Lewis, when you are no longer having to count the steps.[8] It is true that too much freedom and innovation can cause worshipers to lose their balance. Not knowing any of the hymns is a serious impediment to authentic worship. Perhaps some of the best contributions to worship renewal in our day are new texts set to old tunes. Jane Parker Huber and Ruth Duck have made significant contributions in this respect.[9]

The Nature of Humanity

The nature of persons also consists of delicate balances. The first is between humanity as faithful, yet failing. As my colleague Molly Marshall likes to quip, "Our capacity for good is matched only by our capacity for evil." She is right, of course. Even the first pages of the Scriptures portray humanity as created in the image of God, yet sinning.

Walker Percy confirmed this in an informal polling of people. Based on the following two descriptions, he asked, which best describes you?

> A: You are extraordinarily generous, ecstatically loving of the right person, supremely knowledgeable about what is wrong with the country, about people, capable of moments of insight unsurpassed by any scientist or artist or writer in the country. You possess an infinite potentiality.

> B: You are of all people in the world probably the most selfish, hateful, envious (e.g., you take pleasure in reading death notices in the newspaper and in hearing of an acquaintance's heart attack), the most treacherous, the most frightened, and above all the phoniest.[10]

Sixty percent of those polled got it right. They said, "I'm both." That is correct! Humanity is both faithful and failing.

This, too, has profound consequences for worship. The service must strike an appropriate balance between challenge and comfort. Constant condemnation is not fitting in Christian worship, but neither is the omission of opportunity for confession.

The second balance relates to humanity's psychological makeup. Human beings are both rational and emotional in nature. Tragically, worship services typically emphasize either one or the other. "Low church" approaches typically place a premium on immediacy of feelings. Contemporary worshipers want services to touch them, to stir something within them. Balanced worship, however, must seek not only to touch worshipers, but to build mature believers. More important than immediacy of feelings is emotional stability over time.[11] Worship teaches us how to live in the variations of life. Unfortunately, many contemporary approaches are so consumed with praise, there is no place in the service for meditation and confession. "Praise" and "worship" are not synonyms. Worship envelops such things as praise, confession, thanksgiving, encounter, meditation, lamentation, commissioning, and response—to name a few.

"High church" approaches are typically out of balance in respect to a balance of emotions. Worshipers in the more formal traditions rarely experience the emotional range displayed in the Psalms. Knowing full-well how to be silent and repentant, these reflective worshipers rarely experience anything close to ecstasy in worship.

THE NATURE OF THE CHURCH

As with the nature of God and humanity, an understanding of the church consists of balances as well. The first balance is between the church's vertical and horizontal nature. Vertically, those gathered for worship are children of God. Horizontally, they are brothers and sisters in Christ. Both dimensions have implications for worship.

A properly balanced worship service is like a healthy conversation. All of the parties are allowed ample time to speak and to listen. Worship begins, of course, with a word from God. We love, because God loved us first (1 John 4:10). We gather, therefore, in response to what God has done. The first of the great commandments is to love God with our whole selves (Mark 12:28-30). In worship there are moments in which God speaks while we listen (Scripture reading, preaching, baptism, Lord's Supper), and there are moments in which we speak while God listens (prayer, certain responsive readings, and some hymns).

The second great commandment (Mark 12:31) and the horizontal dimension of worship remind us that we also engage one another when we gather to worship. We are to love our neighbor as ourselves in our worship. We sing some hymns addressed to our brothers and sisters in Christ. For instance, there are the older hymns: "Come, All Christians, Be Committed" and "We Are God's People." A newer piece, "The Servant Song," is horizontal as well. It begins:

> We are travelers on a journey
> Fellow pilgrims on the road;
> We are here to help each other
> Walk the mile and bear the load.

The reformation of worship, therefore, is more than a matter of taste. The vertical and horizontal dimensions are both crucial.

The second balance is the tension between God's reign and the world's ways. To worship rightly is to protest the status quo.[12] The Lord's Prayer reminds us that God's will in heaven is not being carried out on earth. We pray for deliverance from this present evil age. Technically, God's reign has begun in Jesus Christ's first coming, but such a reign will not be fully recognized until Jesus comes again. Meanwhile, we gather in worship to protest, to petition God, and to encourage one another in the face of the world's ways.

Observing the Christian year (something now done in both "high church" and some "low church" traditions) is a concrete way of contrasting God's reign with the world's ways. The Christian year begins with the anticipation of Christ's birth, while retail stores advertise end-of-the-year sales. Likewise, 4th of July celebrations in some churches often imply that America is somehow God's favored nation, a notion foreign to the biblical witness. Our theological heritage of independence begins with total dependence on God to deliver Israel out of Egypt (Exod 12) and the ultimate deliverance of the saints through the death of Jesus.

This contrast between the world's ways and God's reign raises an important issue in contemporary worship studies. One of the contemporary "how" questions often asked is: "How can we make our worship services attractive to outsiders?" Such a question, of course, is foreign to the New

Testament's portrayal of worship. The biblical texts were written in a culture much different from ours.

In response to such a question, however, my stock reply is: "Good luck!" Good luck attracting persons outside the Christian faith to a religion whose leader was unfairly crucified. There is nothing all that winsome about a religion whose primary icon is a cross (for example, see Luke 14:25-33). It is attractive only to those who by God's grace have come to see it from a different perspective. Of course, we must welcome strangers into our midst as we would welcome the Christ, but as William Willimon notes, "When you join Rotary, they give you a handshake and a lapel pin. When you join the church, we throw you in the water and half drown you."[13]

CONCLUSION

The Christian writer, Annie Dillard, has written a wonderfully creative piece about worship. Scholars frequently quote bits and pieces of it, but it is the work as a whole that is quite remarkable. Readers familiar with her style know that Dillard is often elusive, refusing to let predictable prose stifle her, when slippery poetic imagery will do. In "An Expedition to the Pole" she weaves together two vastly different subjects to create a parable about the state of worship in our churches today.[14]

The title's reference to the "pole" is about numerous polar expeditions explorers have attempted over the years. She describes the pole itself as "that imaginary point on the Arctic Ocean farthest from land in any direction." In the spiritual realm the pole is "relatively inaccessible," what Dillard calls "the pole of great price."

Scattered reflections about her own worship experiences over the years comprise the other part of the piece. Worship, she writes, is like joining the circus as a dancing bear. Sometimes it is clumsy. We fall down on our forepaws. For instance, there was the service in which "no one, least of all the organist, could find the opening hymn. Then no one knew it. Then no one could sing anyway." She adds that during a time of intercessory prayer, the priest shared about a newborn baby and healthy mother for which the congregation had been praying. The priest interjected: "The woman just kept getting more and more pregnant!" Dillard writes, "How often, how shockingly often, have I exhausted myself in church from the effort to keep from laughing out loud? I often laugh all the way home." She adds:

A high school stage play is more polished than this service we have been rehearsing since the year one. In two thousand years, we have not worked out the kinks. We positively glorify them. Week after week we witness the same miracle: that God is so mighty he can stifle his own laughter. Week after week, we witness the same miracle: that God, for reasons unfathomable, refrains from blowing our dancing bear act to smithereens. Week after week Christ washes the disciples' dirty feet, handles their very toes, and repeats, It is all right—believe it or not—to be people.

Dillard spends pages detailing 19th-century expeditions in which everything that could go wrong did. For example, she tells of a ship that was struck by an enormous ice floe in the Arctic. Most of the crew remained on board, but those left behind drifted 1,300 miles on a floe until they were rescued.

Reading about these expeditions and tales of worship, I begin to sense that there are many parallels: adventure, human ingenuity battling to overcome something bigger than ourselves, and yes, even a certain degree of danger. Dillard asks, "Why do we people in churches seem like cheerful, brainless tourists on a packaged tour of the Absolute?" She describes a ship's crew joining with the tourists in merriment, acting like regular people—everyone assuming someone was minding the ship. She goes on to relate the potential for disaster in this situation to the situation awaiting in church:

> On the whole, I do not find Christians, outside of the catacombs, sufficiently sensible of conditions. Does anyone have the foggiest idea what sort of power we so blithely invoke? Or, as I suspect, does no one believe a word of it? The churches are children playing on the floor with their chemistry sets, mixing up a batch of TNT to kill a Sunday morning. It is madness to wear ladies' straw hats and velvet hats to church; we should all be wearing crash helmets. Ushers should issue life preservers and signal flares; they should lash us to our pews. For the sleeping god may wake someday and take offense, or the waking god may draw us out to where we can never return.

Which way is worship going in the next century? Hopefully, it is going the right way, navigating toward the correct destination. Hopefully, rather than continuing to focus on secondary issues of form and preference, the church will smell the salt air and wake up, feel the waves and recognize the incredible significance of worship. Hopefully, the ship will be righted! May it be so![15]

NOTES

[1]Robert E. Webber, *Evangelicals on the Canterbury Trail* (Wilton CT: Morehouse-Barlow, 1985).

[2]Robert Webber, *Signs of Wonder* (Nashville: Abbott-Martyn, 1992).

[3]See Donald P. Hustad, "Baptist Worship Forms: Uniting the Charleston and Sandy Creek Traditions," *Review and Expositor* 85 (1988): 31-42; and Thomas R. McKibbens, Jr., "Our Baptist Heritage in Worship," *Review and Expositor* 80 (1983):53-69.

[4]Martin E. Marty, "Holy Ground, Sacred Sound," public lecture at Zion Lutheran Church, Portland OR, 14 November 1993, cited by Marva Dawn, *Reaching Out Without Dumbing Down* (Grand Rapids: Eerdmans, 1995) 130.

[5]Thomas C. Oden, ed., *Parables of Kierkegaard* (Princeton: Princeton University Press, 1978) 89-90.

[6]C. Welton Gaddy, *The Gift of Worship* (Nashville: Broadman, 1992) 201.

[7]Carol Doran and Thomas H. Troeger, *Trouble at the Table* (Nashville: Abingdon, 1992) 94-100.

[8]C. S. Lewis, *Letters to Malcom: Chiefly on Prayer* (New York: Harcourt, Brace and World, 1963) 4-5.

[9]For example, see Jane Parker Huber, *Singing in Celebration* (Louisville KY: Westminster/John Knox, 1996); and Ruth C. Duck and Michael G. Bausch, eds., *Everflowing Streams* (New York: Pilgrim, 1981).

[10]Percy Walker, *Lost in the Cosmos* (New York: Farrar, Straus, and Giroux, Inc., 1983).

[11]Dawn, 69-72.

[12]Don E. Saliers, *Worship as Theology* (Nashville: Abingdon, 1994), builds his entire approach to worship on the basis of worship in protest to the status quo and anticipation of Christ's second coming.

[13]William H. Willimon, *Peculiar Speech: Preaching to the Baptized* (Grand Rapids: Eerdmans, 1992) 32.

[14]Annie Dillard, *Teaching a Stone to Talk* (San Francisco: HarperPerennial, 1982) 35-70.

[15]This material was first presented in lecture format to three churches in the St. Louis area in July 1997: Delmar Baptist Church, Deperes Baptist Church, and Second Baptist Church. I am grateful for their participation and encouragement.

THE WATERED GARDEN

DISCIPLESHIP AND STEWARDSHIP IN TOMORROW'S CHURCHES

Larry McKinney

To Robin, who truly knows what stewardship is.

Larry McKinney

They shall come and sing aloud on the height of Zion, and they shall be radiant over the goodness of the Lord, over the grain, the wine, and the oil, and over the young of the flock and the herd; their life shall become like a watered garden, and they shall never languish again. (Jer 31:12)

THE GARDENS OF MEMORY AND DREAMS

EVERYONE HAS A WAY OF CLASSIFYING PEOPLE. As a child, I discovered that persons fell naturally into two groups: those who possessed gardens and those who had only homes. The gardeners, like my grandparents, lived idyllic lives—ebullient Adams and Eves whose industry in the interval between the rising and setting sun was shared in an Eden of sunshine and showers, among verdant crops stretching toward azure skies, and surrounded by the assorted sweet scents God's good earth yields.

Those of us who had only houses seemed somehow dispossessed of this significant birthright. Walls and schedules made us strangers to the seasons, where the year might just as well have been a perpetual winter. Yet God graced me with the opportunity to spend many splendid spring days in the garden with Grandma and Grandpa. It is a garden of memory now (and what pleasant memory), but I return to it often, for it was there that abiding attitudes about the nature of stewardship were formed and fostered.

They are simple attitudes, really, whose tenets God set initially in the garden of Genesis: Creator God loves earth's steadfast stewards endlessly, surrounds them with a bounty of good things, and endows them with hearts for sharing. Humanity's fall turned that garden into a garden of dreams. Still, the precepts of paradise remain, and are as binding as ever, even if they are not lived out perfectly by today's earthbound mortals.

Nowadays as an increasing number of gardenless cyber Christians strive to clear schedules for growth in Christian discipleship, will they find the garden of stewardship? If so, will they see it from a window, or will they become gardeners themselves? The stewards to whom God has entrusted the local churches of today may well hold the seeds of tomorrow's harvest.

THE GARDEN TODAY

I must admit that I am no prophet of tomorrow's trends; attempting to stay abreast of today's is challenge enough. In years past, information was a scarce commodity, and the search for it involved both time and skill. Today's skill entails sifting from among a plethora of readily available information for the right data, and quickly. What my exploration into current Christian stewardship has uncovered may surprise no one. Quite possibly, it will merely confirm what Christian leaders have already discovered.

There has been a 27-year decline in the percentage of income that Christians give to churches and ministry organizations. Only 2-3 Christians out of 10 give 10% or more of their incomes to churches or ministry organizations. Gifts from about 5% of contributors account for about 50% of a ministry's income, and gifts from about 10% of contributors make up close to 75% of an average church's or organization's revenues.[1]

Moreover, there has been a proliferation of Christian para-church groups and secular nonprofit organizations during the last four decades. More and more of them are employing bright and creative specialists in fund-raising. These organizations are availing themselves of the latest marketing technologies, including direct mail (now dubbed "snail mail"), the internet, and telemarketing. These techniques allow them to reach vast numbers of people while appearing to present a personal touch.

In the face of such sophisticated fund-raising promotions, the local church's "pass the offering plate" approach might seem passé. It should not, for recent trends also indicate that some exciting stewardship opportunities are in store for local churches.

PLANTING TIME FOR THE LOCAL CHURCH

The average Christian now receives 25-100 fund-raising appeals in a year.[2] Thus, not only must Christians now seek to avoid the many deceptive and fraudulent organizations, they are faced also with considering the cases of an overwhelming array of worthy causes. The net result is that many Christians admit to feeling besieged, if not burned out, by fund-raising appeals. Who presently does not keep a "reasons I cannot give" speech rehearsed and ready? Still, current data show that the average Christian will donate to at least four organizations in a year, with the local church receiving priority.[3]

How is this good news for local churches? First, the local church is one ministry that truly does relate personally to its constituents. This means that it can include and involve Christians actively in its ministries. Many other ministries are unable to do this, as in the case of a number of those whose reach is through mass-marketing. A recent study shows what ministers have sensed for some time: the more involved a member is in church life, the greater will be that person's level of stewardship.[4]

A second portion of good news arises from the first. Because churches involve members actively in ministries, they can help Christians grow in the discipline of stewardship by allowing them to give of their talents and time, as well as of their money. Lyle Schaller has pointed out that church members are becoming more diverse in their backgrounds and lifestyles. Therefore, opportunities for involving them now "need to be numerous and diverse."[5]

If involvement and diversity are important keys in engendering a stewardship lifestyle, then how are churches doing in utilizing them? My own informal survey among pastors, seminary faculty members, and seminarians indicates a desire for improvement and an openness to new approaches. Further queries have given me the impression that stewardship is generally a silent subject in many seminaries, Christian colleges, denominations, and churches.

More than a few ministers have told me that their churches currently have no established programs for teaching Christian stewardship. Others have related that they have only a limited program set to coincide with the period of pledging to the church's annual budget.

It came as no surprise when a majority of the church persons I spoke with told me that they equate stewardship with church bills, buildings, and budgets. Yet, I have found most of them open to broadening their understandings, as long as the methods in no way resemble some of the past guilt-driven approaches.

So, the promised land of change is at hand, with many gardens to be planted. In the garden of stewardship, church leaders will have ample opportunity to invite Christians into the sunshine of sharing through new programs. The goal is to enhance the progress of God's kingdom through the local church, whose members are lifelong stewards of their talents, time, and money. The time to plant is now. God's garden awaits its faithful stewards, and so does immeasurable joy.

PLANTING FOR THE GLORY OF GOD

In order for the garden to yield, it must be weeded continually of such dishonorable approaches as prey on guilt and selfishness. To be sure, Christians have seen enough poor examples of so-called stewardship theology. They run the spectrum from the theology of poverty to that of prosperity. Not unlike two forms of ancient gnosticism, one extreme regards ownership as a curse, while the other views increasing wealth as the divine reward of tithing.

The fruitful church stewardship program will inspire Christians to make matters of personal stewardship a joyous and lifelong discipline to be prayerfully considered and cultivated year after year. To accomplish this, the program must be theologically sound, hence biblically based.

The biblically based program will thrive if given a perennial place within the church's educational, worship, and outreach ministries. Continuity, comprehensiveness, and creativity are all important elements in assuring a bountiful harvest—not only in the lives of individual Christians and in the community life of the church, but most significantly for the glory of God.

THE ASSURANCE OF BOUNTY

I once read the fascinating account of an archaeologist who, while excavating among Anasazi ruins in New Mexico, found a basket containing seeds more than seven centuries old. On a whim he planted a few seeds, and to his surprise plants actually began to spring up.

The past may well be the most fertile place to find tomorrow's church stewardship program. The precepts and caveats presented in the Bible—from the primeval garden to the early Christian experience—are both numerous and telling concerning the future of sharing.

Locating biblical passages that speak to stewardship is not a difficult task. Topical and study Bibles, some of which are available now for computer, can be of assistance. Recently I spoke with a woman who is working on a project to produce the first ever Stewardship Study Bible. She is employed as a fund-raiser for a para-church missions organization.

The above prompts a word of advice. If Christians have the impression that stewardship is primarily about money—and I have found this largely to be the case—it is because print materials, programs, and persons have led them to conclude that. It is the task of ministers, church leaders, and fund-raisers to help Christians see a much broader perspective.

Only when the subject of money is blended appropriately along with the other elements comprising the soil of servanthood will tomorrow's Christians quicken to the call to the garden of God. More than one stewardship program has faltered from the first by focusing on money altogether. Too many of them have left Christians riddled with feelings of guilt and burden.

The Psalmist asked, "What shall I return to the Lord for all his bounty to me?" (Ps 116:12). A burning sense of shame transforms an offering of any kind into an unenthusiastic obligation. A grateful heart renders glad gifts that are as sincerely offered as they are assorted in type.

The Harvest

Here is the salient point: the goal of Christian stewardship is to glorify God. Stewardship's byproduct is spiritual growth, both within individuals and among the body of believers. The program of stewardship, then, is nothing other than a framework for involving Christians in experiencing God's glory and bounty more fully, and through means by which they could not otherwise experience them.

In the face of such intangibles, is it possible to measure a program's achievements? From the human side, only insofar as transformed lives bear witness to God's glory and bounty. Counting income can be an inaccurate indicator—remember the story of the poor widow's mite (Mark 12:42-42; Luke 21:2-4). Still, certain hallmarks distinguish the well-founded program and assure that its harvest will be plentiful.

First, the well-founded program will prompt Christians to remember that God is the owner of everything. One fine morning in May of 1877, General Oliver Howard summoned a defiant Nez Percè tribal leader named Toohoolhoolzote to Fort Lapwai on the Idaho Indian reservation. General Howard's intent was to persuade Toohoolhoolzote that it would be in the best interest of the Nez Percè nation to move from its ancestral homeland to the reservation. A devout Christian, General Howard believed he was doing God's will in showing the leader the many advantages of reservation life. As the parley progressed, the general grew so annoyed at Toohoolhoolzote's arguments against the plan that he finally told the Nez Percè leader to "shut up." Toohoolhoolzote responded: "Who are you? Are you the Great Spirit? Did you make the world? Did you make the rivers to run for us to drink? Did you make the grass to grow? Did you make all these things, that you talk to us as though we are children?"[6] General Howard could think of no better reply than to place Toohoolhoolzote under arrest.

"The earth is the Lord's and all that is in it" (Ps 24:1). The stewardship program that commences with this truth will help Christians understand that they are transitory trustees of God's eternal order. Psalm 24 is no "it goes without saying" statement, for history testifies that human yearnings for ownership run deep.

The apostle Paul recited Psalm 24 to the Corinthian Christians, along with the sage advice to "think about others and not about ourselves" (1 Cor 10:24 CEV). It is no small calling to be the caretakers of creation and the stewards of equity.

A second hallmark of the fruitful program is that it will encourage Christians to grow spiritually and in their reliance on God. In 2 Corinthians 8 and 9, Paul exhorts Christians to excel in generosity. He writes, "The one who sows sparingly will also reap sparingly, and the one who sows bountifully will also reap bountifully. . . . And God is able to provide you with every blessing in abundance, so that . . . you may share abundantly in every good work" (9:6, 8). Paul had a particular good work in mind—a collection for the church in Jerusalem, whose followers faced destitution. The blessing came as gentile Christians forged new bonds of unity with Jewish Christians. This marked a pivotal moment in the growth of early Christianity and is an indispensable lesson for modern Christians. Ethnic diversification will be an increasing issue for American Christianity. By the turn of the 21st century, fully half of an average assembly will be non-Caucasian. The spirit of sharing presents enormous possibilities for forging a new American mosaic.

A third distinctive of the program of substance is that it will bring the wisdom of God to bear upon the lives of Christians living in a culture of materialism. The temptation to prefer possessions and physical comforts to the divine spiritual values faces Christians today as much as it did the prototypical humans of Eden. Preachers preach on it, prophets have prophesied against it, and Jesus uttered discourses of reproof concerning it. In the Parable of the Rich Fool (Luke 12:13-21), Jesus delivers a particularly "hard" saying on worldly prosperity, yet one that speaks clearly to contemporary Christians—"So it is with those who store up treasures for themselves but are not rich toward God" (v. 21). It is no coincidence that the ensuing passage contains Jesus' counsel to his disciples not to worry about material things, but rather to "make sure your treasure is safe in heaven" (v. 33, CEV).

Lastly, the well-founded stewardship program will strengthen the stability and ministries of the local church. I am touched by the stories of our seminarians. Of course, each has come to Central Seminary in answer to a call from God. Yet, what amazes me continually is the extent of self-sacrifice.

Some have left substantial careers, where financial advancement and prestige were assured. Most, by choosing ministry careers, are forgoing much of the promise of future monetary reward. Our ministers come to our churches as servants with hearts inclined to service over affluence, and are deserving of our best stewardship.

A great miracle happened more than nineteen centuries ago. Members of the early Christian community began to share "everything they had with each other" (Acts 4:32, CEV). By that, God began to show them, and us, the means by which God's bounty is multiplied.[7] Make no mistake, this is neither metaphor nor Marxist maxim. It is the work of the Holy Spirit in the lives of God's faithful. What a powerful witness it must have put forth in the largely non-Christian ancient Mediterranean world! What a witness it can bear today!

The joy of the garden of stewardship resides in those churches wherein Christians give gladly of their talents, time, and possessions. Not long ago a pastor told me of his church's plan to launch a much-needed new ministry. Upon hearing of it, many members immediately gave funds to undergird the program. Yet in the end, the ministry could not be undertaken, because no volunteers could be found to offer their talents and time.

At Central Seminary we have witnessed the miracle of stewardship both through monetary gifts from our faithful friends and by way of a marvelous volunteers program. We are blessed continually by the many individuals and church groups who assist us in countless campus projects. If we had been required to pay for their services during a recent two-year period, it would have cost the seminary more than $500,000. Through this program our financial donors and others literally can see how gifts are multiplied to the glory of God. I pray that it is so in your church as well.

In the Garden of Hope

Pity poor Jeremiah. The prophetic mantel could not have fallen on him at a more unpropitious moment. The year 627 B.C. found Judah as vassals of the arrogant Assyrians, and over the next four decades matters would only worsen. The equally haughty Babylonians would invade Jerusalem not once, but twice, destroying the Temple and deporting to Babylon many of Jeremiah's surviving kinfolk.

Eventually the prophet found himself in exile in Egypt, yet alive and with a host of messages from the Lord awaiting delivery. Not all of the words were dismaying. Into the very heart of the displaced Judahites' hour of hopelessness Jeremiah conveyed God's promise of restoration. He spread it tirelessly like the balm of Gilead on homesick souls languishing by the rivers of Babylon. The children of Judah had become gardeners in that land (Jer 29:5, 28), but each sunset no doubt found them gazing far beyond their gardens to the western horizon.

There is something in the notion of a promised land that refuses to die. Even now it is so. And those who seek it will find it, for it is not far away. What remains is for it to be transformed into a land of promise. The garden of hope awaits its stewards.

> *May the stewards' vista broaden yet beyond the gardens of this earth. May God grant each gardener the grander vision of a new garden of paradise, girded by four soft-flowing streams, and nurtured by mists that descend from amethystine hills, where all that is planted flourishes amidst winterless years and yields in abundance, so that at the transfiguration of the twilight hour the happy steward may praise the Lord and say, "My soul is like a watered garden."*

Notes

[1]Scott Preissler, "The Introduction to Stewardship," a seminar presented by the Christian Stewardship Association, Kansas City MO, September 1997.

[2]Brian Kluth, "The Good News/Bad News about the Winds of Change in Stewardship Trends," in *Church Stewardship Resource Kit* (Milwaukee WI: Christian Stewardship Association, 1997) 4.

[3]George Barna, "Recent Trends in Christian Stewardship," an address presented at the annual summit of the Christian Stewardship Association, Kansas City MO, September 1997.

[4]Dean R. Hoge, Charles E. Zech, Patrick H. McNamara, and Michael J. Donahue, "Who Gives to the Church and Why," *Christian Century*, vol. 13, no. 35 (4 December 1996) 1199.

[5]Ibid.

[6]Henry Woodhead, ed., *The American Indians: People of the Western Range* (Richmond VA: Time-Life Books, 1995) 153.

[7]An excellent, and oft-overlooked, stewardship passage with which to pair this pericope of Acts 4:32-37 is the miracle of the Feeding of the Five Thousand (Luke 9:10-17).

CHANGES AND CHALLENGES

THE CHURCH AND MISSIONS
AT THE TURN OF THE CENTURY

Robert E. Fulop

[signature]

"ANXIETY GROWS AS 2000 DRAWS NEAR—Millennium is bringing with it an astonishing set of predictions, fears, and just plain nonsense." So notes a headline in the August 31, 1997 issue of the *Kansas City Star*. Fears of more deadly earthquakes; volcanoes; stellar episodes; wars and killings; computer, boat, and airplane crashes; and various religious predictions are on some peoples' minds. There were similar concerns when the new millennium approached in 1000 A.D.

As the church faces the 21st century with its far-reaching changes, what realities can we foresee? Is the church aware of the globalization of Christianity today and the many changes it is bringing? What plans will the different churches make as they face the 21st century? Will we stay faithful to the mission of our Lord? Will we open our eyes to the realities of the changes, and adapt and prepare ourselves to meet the challenges?

This chapter will explore the present reality of global Christianity, the global challenges, and global churches' commitments in preparation for the turn of the century.

GLOBAL CHRISTIANITY

Among the historic events of the 20th century is the growth of Christianity outside of Europe and North America. As missionaries in large numbers from both mainline agencies and faith missions spread throughout the open countries of the world immediately after World War II, Christianity took root. Many churches and educational institutions sprang up in Asia, Latin America, Africa, and Oceania. In spite of 18th-century Enlightenment philosophy that ruled supreme with its attendant rationalism, Christianity's heart withstood its cold hand. It planted the seed of the gospel in response to the biblical teaching of Christ, his apostles, and the apostle Paul.

Barriers to the spread of Christianity were many. Some denominations, dominated by a theology of total dependence on God to evangelize the world, withdrew into their comfortable local churches and let the world pass by. Some churches, beset with problems of decline, gave little or nominal support to missions. Others felt that missions should give way to an emphasis on accommodation to world religions and cooperate with them.[2] Some churches, having supported missions through the 1960s, began to shift responsibilities to the national churches to do their own evangelism with the hope that there would be no need for sending more Western missionaries. One author, after indicating a 45.2% decrease in the number of American Baptist missionaries between 1953 and 1973, commented:

> Perhaps the greater significance of the missionary force should be seen in the vast increase of full-time church workers [overseas]—up 152.9%—and in the increased number of total Christian workers—up 43.1%.[3]

Many concluded that the day of sending missionaries from North America and Europe was over.

In addition to decreased support of overseas missions by denominations and individual churches, there were other barriers to the expansion of the gospel: attrition of missionaries overseas, lack of finances at home, and closure of programs in theological seminaries for the specific training of missionaries.

In spite of barriers, Christianity gradually emerged as a worldwide force, but it was no longer numerically centered in the West. By 1986, there were more Christians in Africa, Asia, Oceania, and Latin America than in the West.[4] In fact, the growth of Christianity outside the West continues today while church attendance and vitality in Europe are declining. Churches in the West give evidence of "old age" with its attendant deficiencies while the churches in the East and South exhibit "youth" with all of its energy, expectancy, vigor, and hope. Everywhere there are new challenges from other religions and a new secularism that keep creative minorities of Christians sharp and alert to explain their faith and Christian practice.

One evidence of the reality and vitality of global Christianity is the increasing production of writings by third world theologians. No longer do missionaries write commentaries and theology from Western points of view. This activity by missionaries was needed in the early years of mission, but by the end of World War II it was apparent that if Christianity was to be communicated by local Christian leaders, it had to be explained in the context of the thinking of the nationals. Non-Western peoples must develop their understanding of Christ and his Lordship in terms of their own culture. In most cases this development takes place in cultures where the majority of people are nonbelievers and Western missionaries are still welcome but in a new servant role.

Third world theologians began their own Ecumenical Association of Third World Theologians in 1976, meeting in Tanzania. Since then they have met in India (1981), Mexico (1986), and Africa (1992).[5] Papers from these conferences were printed in English and serve to raise questions for interaction with the West and among other third world countries. This dialogue is bound to stimulate global Christianity to consider new approaches in evangelizing newly mobile populations in the West and throughout the world. Western churches particularly need to benefit from these emerging trends as they face new immigrant neighbors from Asian, African, and Latin American countries.

Possibly the best way to understand the shift in global Christianity is to understand the new phenomena of third world missions. Early in the 19th century, missionaries from Oceania were sent to various islands to communicate the gospel. They were highly successful, but few outsiders knew of their success. In 1972, James Wong, Peter Larsen, and Dwight Pentecost indicated that 3,404 missionaries had been sent from third world countries. In 1980, the estimate was 13,000.[6] That number had increased to 35,924 in 1989. If the growth of the number of third world missionaries continues as it grew between 1972 and 1989, there will be more than 136,000 missionaries from Asia, Latin America, Africa, and Oceania by the year 2000.[7] While the West is ambivalent and sometimes negative regarding the need to continue sending missionaries, developing countries are finding ways of sending out missionaries. An illustration of this missionary zeal is Korea.

In 1900, when there were no overseas Korean missionaries, only 0.5% of Korea was Christian. Today, when Korea has missionaries in a large number of countries around the world, the Korean population is 35.3% Christian.[8] Since 1989, Korean missionaries have established 50 congregations in Moscow alone. When, in 1979, a Korean student announced to the World Mission Fellowship at Central Baptist Theological Seminary that Korea was willing and able to supplant America as a missionary-sending country, I was stunned by what I thought was arrogance. Today I accept his voice as prophetic not only of Korea but other sending churches in Africa, Latin America, Asia, and Oceania.

In the truest sense of the word, Christianity has become global. The gospel has not only spread throughout the globe, but its seed has produced churches that are also missionary-sending churches. In some ways these churches are similar to the churches of the first three centuries. Growth, vital witness, social involvement, and martyrdom characterize these churches.

Today, while persecution has almost been eliminated from the West, it is on the rise in third world countries. David Barrett calculates that in 1900 there were 35,000 martyrs worldwide, but the projection for 1997 was 160,000, and 300,000 by 2025.[9] In northeastern Nigeria, a Christian was arrested by Hausa officials. In front of the villagers he was charged: "Pastor Selchun was carrying a Christian Bible!" His punishment was to have his right hand cut off. After the sword severed the hand, with great anguish he raised his left hand and sang, "He is Lord, He is Lord. He has risen from the dead, and He is Lord." Pastor Selchun was only one of 60,000 Christians made homeless when they were driven away by violent mobs. Over a three-month period, 100 churches were torched, and 300 Christians were put to death.[10] We can reasonably expect that Tertullian's words, "The blood of the martyrs is the seed of the church," will continue in the future to describe the Christian church.

What are we to make of these vibrant, dedicated, persecuted, and growing churches? Could it be, as Bob Sjogren observed, that "today, mounting evidence forces us to acknowledge that North America has been largely bypassed by the great spiritual harvest occurring in other parts of the world?"[11] Lack of communication leaves most of the North American churches unaware of what God is doing in our world. Perhaps if we knew and interacted with more overseas Christians, we in the West would be better able to embrace the future and respond to the Holy Spirit's direction.

GLOBAL CHALLENGES

No longer can we only think locally. Everything with which we come into contact indicates a global connection. Much of the food we eat comes from Latin America or even Australia. Electronics, automobiles, and many essentials come from Asia, especially China and Japan. Increasingly, more of our neighbors are immigrants from Africa, Latin America, and Asia. Global connections have brought about economic and ideological challenges for all, particularly Christians whose numbers are decreasing in the West while other religions gain numerically. As the church enters the 21st century, it must redefine its mission.

For the last 100 years, Christianity has claimed only about 34% of the world's population. Barrett projects a growth to 36.9% by 2025.[12] If

Christianity is growing in non-Western countries, why has the percentage stayed relatively the same? Two reasons may be suggested.

(1) Europe has consistently registered a decline. Germany has registered a dramatic decline since the unification of East and West Germany. According to an article in *The Christian Century,* "While 50% of residents from western Germany claim to be religious, only 1 in 5 East Germans makes the same claim, producing a national average of fewer than half of all citizens."[13] Other European countries register similar losses due to secularism and indifference. The West has become a mission field, as Leslie Newbigin has suggested. His concern was taken seriously especially in North America where several years ago a number of interested persons formed the "Gospel and Our Culture Network" (GOCN).[14]

(2) While third world missions has registered a rapid increase of missionaries, North American and European mainline denominations have succumbed to pressures and a reinterpretation of mission that have paralyzed their sending efforts. Only independent and evangelical denominations register gains in sending large numbers of missionaries today.[15] If this loss of nerve in the West for missions continues, Christianity's spread will continue but at a slower pace.

In the last ten years many Christians have become concerned about world religions. If Christianity is about a third of the world population, how are we to think of God's relationship to non-Christian religions? Before we attempt an answer, let us look at the statistics of the World Religions.

• Muslims—1.1 billion
• Hindus—806 million
• Buddhists—328 million
• tribal religionists—100 million
• Sikhs—20 million
• Jews—14 million

Counting atheists and new religionists, there are about 3.8 billion non-Christians in a world population of 5.8 billion today.[16]

While the debate about God's relationship to non-Christians has been going on since biblical times, it has become acute in our generation. Theologians have taken sides basically within three groups: Exclusivists, Inclusivists, and Pluralists.[17]

Exclusivists believe that salvation is limited to the atoning action of the triune God known only in the life, death, and resurrection of Jesus Christ.

Acts 4:12 is cited as clear evidence that only through Christ can anyone be saved. "There is salvation in no one else, for there is no other name under heaven given among mortals by which we must be saved." Some Exclusivists hold that God in God's mysterious action may elect some to salvation who have never heard the gospel, but this is not the way God normally intends salvation.

The great theologian of the 20th century, Karl Barth, defined Exclusivism by writing that religion cannot provide salvation. Only God brings humankind to salvation through the revelation of Christ. Religions, even the greatest, are merely humankind's attempt to reach God. In other words, there is a fundamental discontinuity because of human sin entering the equation. Only through God's gracious revelation in the incarnation of Christ can humankind approach God.[18]

Inclusivists maintain that God's mercy extends to people of other religions. They cite Scripture passages as evidence.

- "He himself was not the light, but he came to testify to the light. The true light, which enlightens everyone, was coming into the world" (John 1:8-9).
- "He has not left himself without a witness in doing good—giving you rains from heaven and fruitful seasons" (Acts 14:17).
- "[God] desires everyone to be saved and to come to the knowledge of the truth" (1 Tim 2:4).

Roman Catholics have dealt with the issue of exclusivism as a result of the Second Vatican Council (1962–1965). They now recognize Christians of other churches as recipients of God's gifts and graces, and some of their theologians extend this recognition to non-Christian religions. For example, they believe that if Buddhists are true followers and live up to the teachings of Buddha, they may be drawn closer to God. Similarly, some Protestants believe that members of world religions should be accepted as "pre-Christians" or even as "anonymous Christians." This does not mean that the finality of Christ is eclipsed, but rather that Christ is the criterion of salvation wherever it is proposed.

Inclusivists affirm the need to witness to the truth in Jesus Christ and hope that through acceptance of others, they may be brought through the mysterious work of the Holy Spirit to the acceptance of Christ as the fulfillment of God's ultimate plan for humankind. Exclusivists would not accept the part of the Inclusivist view that affirms continuity with non-Christian religions nor their attempt to simultaneously affirm God's redeeming gifts in both non-Christian religions and Christianity.[19] Certainly, Exclusivists would not accept the openness of Pluralists.

Pluralists applaud the Inclusivists for accepting the world's great religions as institutions, but go beyond that by admitting non-Christian religions as equal partners in the common quest of God. They begin by asserting that all knowledge of God is conditioned by our human condition. All religions can contribute understanding of God and neighbor from their own experiences. All religions developed in isolation. Because of the shrinkage of the world, all religions need to enter into a dialogue to share their insights. For some Pluralists, this may lead to a convergence of world religions in some type of wider ecumenism, but most Pluralists reject such liberal inclusivism because it completely relativizes Jesus Christ. On the basis that God will judge us by our service to others and our faithfulness to God, Pluralists downplay the need for confession of Christ as the only Savior and Lord.[20]

While the three views of Christianity's approach to world religions offer a perspective on the problem, they tend to isolate Christians into three groups, which in the final analysis do not fully characterize them. For example, Exclusivists are too harshly relegated to a group that is narrow, negative, uncaring, intolerant, and devoid of love for others. Yet, this group sacrifices the most by sending missionaries with holistic emphases on ministry. Inclusivists suffer from the ambiguity of affirming the institutional acceptance of non-Christian religions while asserting Christianity's uniqueness as found in Jesus Christ. The Pluralists' approach lacks a historical perspective of Christian doctrinal development and too easily dismisses Martin Luther's emphasis on justification by faith. Even though their insistence on Christians engaging people of other religions in open-ended dialogue risks relativizing Jesus, the dialogue is necessary as required by scripture and the early church's literature.[21]

The challenge for Christians today is to appreciate the thinking of various religions and to use it in witnessing for Christ. Another challenge is the global perspective of missions.

No longer does the missionary enterprise have one center as it did in the 19th and early 20th centuries. As Christianity moved from Jerusalem to Europe and North America, the center was easily identifiable. Now the center of missions includes not only the places receiving missionaries, but any place where churches send missionaries. For example, while Western missionaries work in Korea, Korean missionaries sent to America work with immigrant Koreans, African-Americans, and Caucasians. Because of this global perspective, it is impossible to discuss the meaning of mission only from a Western point of view.

The challenge of missions for the 21st century is to take globalization seriously and change its approach to the remaining task of world evangelization. The terms mission, evangelism, and witness take on new meanings. Average church members would give the following definitions: Mission is sending missionaries overseas to communicate Christ; evangelism is sharing the gospel so that people will believe; and witness is telling one's personal experience with Jesus Christ. Because the world situation has changed, we must change the emphasis on mission. It is not simply reshaping other cultures and/or negating other religions; it is living the Christian faith in the presence of others. Accordingly, evangelism would respond to questions of why Christians live as they do, and witness would mean the living of a compassionate Christian life.[22]

Most missionaries today do not put the issue in such opposites. Rather, missionaries are sent to different cultures and respond according to the situation. If missionaries engage in dialogue with persons of other religions in order to understand and communicate the gospel, evangelism is communicating the faith. But evangelism also entails giving answers to people who ask about the meaning of the Christian faith. Witness may mean the living out of one's faith in the presence of others while seeking opportunities to witness to the redemptive power of the resurrected Christ in their lives.

The question is: What challenges are coming from the globalization of missions? What are Asia, Africa, Latin America, and Oceania learning about their own mission that challenges the Western definition and practice of mission? While there are some influences apparent today, the 21st century will increasingly reflect a greater interaction between various religions, thus resulting in an enrichment of the meaning of mission. A few examples may be considered.

Kosuke Koyama, has rightly proposed that the crusading spirit in missions found in some missionaries needs to be changed into a crucifying spirit or mentality.[23] Missionaries in the past have been criticized for the triumphal spirit in their approach to non-Christian peoples. While most missionaries are aware of the crusading image and adopt the crucified servant attitude, many church people still idolize missionaries and unconsciously promote the crusading image.

One of the great problems among Western missionaries is the extent that individualism has hampered mission work. Individualism arose from the American frontier and appears in varied forms in American people today, including missionaries. Team ministries consequently appear to be in trouble because of this excessive individualism.

In a perceptive article written by Joshua K. Ogawa, several suggestions from an Asian perspective are offered. The most helpful contribution to the global challenge to mission thinking is what Asians can contribute toward solidarity in mission. Take, for example, the strong connection of the Asian person to the home churches. There is a loyalty of missionaries to churches and churches to missionaries that is lacking in the West today.[24] Also, while "groupism"—including decision by consensus found especially in Japan— can lead to stifling individual initiative, it has much to teach missionaries on how to work together to achieve mission goals.[25]

Third world countries challenge us to reassess the effects of Western missions on their churches. Far too often the Western missionary and agency have created a dependent situation. This dependence has done harm to both the missionary and the church. To the missionary, it has given a dangerous sense of control. To the church, it has resulted in immobilization. The two sides are now in dialogue and are making gradual progress in solving the problem. The challenge will be to forge a partnership in mission that will mobilize the dependent church for mission and maintain a continuing servant mentality for the sending church as together they keep the task of mission in mutual focus.[26]

The challenge of the poor continues to reshape the concept of mission. Latin America, through its liberation theologians, has drawn the attention of the world to the poor. Because the poor are also found in Africa and parts of Asia, what Latin America has discussed is valid for the global understanding of mission. Preferential consideration needs to be given to the poor in mission objectives, and Western missionaries need to deal courageously with missionary affluence. If the preferential option for the poor is demanding attention because there are more poor in the world to be reached for Christ, how can missionaries saturated in affluence relate to the poor in true communication? Jonathan Bonk has caused us to take seriously the problems of affluence and poverty in the dawning 21st century.[27] It is not a new problem but one that increasingly takes on a higher priority in mission discussions.

GLOBAL CHURCHES' COMMITMENTS

The 21st century will demand of the church a fresh interpretation of scripture as it relates to the subject of missions. The church has been guilty in the past of interpreting the Scriptures from only the perspective of its local needs. For example, one pastor preached on the book of Acts without relating its contents to the great, rapid spread of the gospel in the Roman Empire and its continued spread throughout the world today. Others have seized on social issues of legitimate concern and used biblical texts to undergird these causes. Such approaches may be acceptable for meeting the specific challenges of the church in a local area, but they do no justice to the need for considering issues from a global perspective as the Bible demands.

We are all aware of the basic biblical texts that are the foundations for continuing mission in the world. Matthew 28, Acts 1:8, and the book of Jonah stand out. But modern scholarship has called attention to the fact that both the Old Testament and the New Testament cannot be adequately understood without a global perspective. David Bosch offers an affirmation and a warning:

> Our conclusion is that both Old and New Testaments are permeated with the idea of mission. . . . (But) not everything we call mission is indeed mission . . . It is the perennial temptation of the Church to become (a club of religious folklore). . . . The only remedy for this mortal danger lies in challenging herself unceasingly with the true biblical foundations of mission.[28]

In teaching missiology, one must deal with God's relationship to the nations of the world from the first chapters of Genesis throughout the entire Old Testament. An appropriate understanding of Jesus' and Paul's missions cannot be possible unless both the Old Testament texts and the history of the Jewish people's response to God's election of them for mission is clearly understood.

Regarding the New Testament, texts that have been interpreted to yield one truth must be reexamined. For example, the incident where Jesus chases the money-changers from the court of the Gentiles of the temple has always been interpreted to mean a cleansing of the corrupt practices found around the temple. But the real thrust here is that Jesus chose the court of the Gentiles to show how the Jews disregarded their mission to the world by denying the Gentiles entrance even in the court that was reserved for them (Mark 11:15-17). Other texts of the Gospels cry out for interpretation that would put into perspective a new commitment to global missions. Similarly, Paul's letters cannot be studied and explained without acknowledging that all of them were written in a missionary situation.

For a commitment to missions in the 21st century, a careful reexamination of the biblical texts must be made. Providentially, Western churches are no longer the only source of biblical interpretation. Churches in Asia, Africa, Latin America, and Oceania are discovering the missiological thrust from their experiences and thought patterns. Together, Christians can enter the 21st century with greater commitment to Christ, the Lord of mission.

It is no wonder that the bibliography of writings on mission in the Bible has expanded to take into account contributions from missionaries and nationals from the third world. One example is that of Lucien Legrand. While not a national from the third world, he is a veteran missionary in India. His work on the biblical basis of mission not only is an example of biblical scholarship, but is one reflecting the understanding of Scripture from the Hindu background.[29]

The late South African missiologist, David Bosch, summarized the results of his extensive biblical studies in his book, *Transforming Mission*. In it are references and commentary on third world and Western publications on the Bible and mission.[30] In his book, *Mission on the Way*, Charles Van Engen carries the ideas of Bosch further and suggests following themes of God's mission through the Bible as ways of leading to fresh studies on the Bible as authoritative for mission.[31]

In addition to reexaming the biblical texts, there must be a new commitment to mission education in the churches as we face the 21st century. Just as Bible studies that do not reflect new understandings of God's mission will be inadequate for the challenges of the 21st century, so will mission education that does not convey the new global challenges to all levels of education. Our world has so contracted and our societies become so interdependent, we cannot withhold information of what God's mission is doing in the world today.

Traditionally, the Sunday church school has been entrusted with these responsibilities. Mission education must permeate the whole congregation, however. The pastor as leader of mission has a strategic role to fulfill. The pastor's sermons must reflect the biblical themes of mission and prepare people for commitment to mission tasks that are relevant to the world's needs. Mission committees have the opportunity to educate church members. In preparation for special offerings, mission education could further motivate and stimulate those who are expected to give.

One of the best ways of educating a congregation is by visits of members to mission areas. Reporting on a mission experience is an excellent way of spreading the news among peers about what is happening in missions today. Of special value in the educative process are short-term missionaries who serve from three months to three years.[32] Upon return to their home churches, these people can educate lay people and offer inspiration and vitality that cannot be conveyed through formal education mediums. With computer capabilities available to a wider audience, the opportunity to be informed by mission websites supported by denominational or educational centers can be of invaluable service to persons committed to mission.

Beyond contributing money and being involved in short-term missionary projects, people can be involved in missions by being "welcomers" to international students in universities and schools. Many of these students will be the future leaders of their countries. Who knows what the significance of a converted student or one who has been befriended by Christians will be in the future.[33] Increasingly, as members of world religions emigrate to the West, the witness of welcoming should be encouraged. God has brought them next door to us to provide us with opportunities to be engaged in mission without going overseas.[34]

The 21st century will call for a greater commitment by global Christians. Commitment to sending out missionaries will increase in the third world. Will the segments of Western Christianity with declining interest in sending missionaries face the 21st century with determination to match the enthusiasm of third world missionaries, or will mission interest in the third world surpass that of Western countries?

CONCLUSION

The church faces a new opportunity in the 21st century to influence the world for Christ. Will it recognize the reality of global Christianity today? Will it accept the challenges to mission and move into the 21st century with new commitment, or will it stand at the door of the 21st century satisfied with its past victories and its present limited, local ministry? A church cannot face the future as a viable community of the faithful unless it is renewed by mission. The Jewish philosopher and biblical scholar, Martin Buber, best characterized the Christian faith in the following words:

> Christianity begins as diaspora and mission. The mission means in this case not just diffusion; it is the life-breath of the community and accordingly the basis of the new People of God.[35]

One of the world-renowned supporters of missions near the turn of the 19th century expressed well what the church entering the 21st century needs to hear again. Bishop Selwyn of England warned the church of his day:

It seems to be an indisputable fact that however inadequate a church may be to its own internal wants, it must on no account suspend its missionary duties; that this is in fact the circulation of its life's blood, which would lose its vital power if it never flowed forth to the extremities, but curdled at the heart.[36]

NOTES

[1]David B. Barrett, "Annual Statistical Table on Global Mission: 1990," *International Bulletin of Missionary Research*, 14 (January 1990) 26-27. See also Norman Cohn, *The Pursuit of the Millennium* (Fairlawn NJ: Essential Books, 1957)

[2]William Ernest Hocking, *Rethinking Missions* (New York: Harper and Brothers, 1932) 29-48.

[3]Dean R. Kirkwood, *Seeing Mission Today* (Valley Forge PA: International Ministries, n.d.) 21-22.

[4]David B. Barrett, "Annual Statistical Table on Global Mission: 1986," *International Bulletin of Missionary Research*, 10 (January 1986) 23.

[5]K. C. Abraham and Bernadette Mbuy-Beya, eds., *Spirituality of the Third World* (Maryknoll NY: Orbis, 1994) 207-208.

[6]Lawrence Keyes, *The Last Age of Missions* (Pasadena CA: William Carey Library, 1983) 61.

[7]Larry D. Pate, *From Every People* (Monrovia CA: Marc, 1989) 51. See also Larry D. Pate and Lawrence E. Keyes, "Emerging Missions in a Global Church," *International Bulletin of Missionary Research*, 10 (October 1986) 156-61.

[8]Patrick Johnstone, *Operation World* (Grand Rapids: Zondervan, 1993) 336-37. See also David B. Barrett, *World Christian Encyclopedia* (Oxford: Oxford University Press, 1982) 441; and Stan Guthrie, "Korean Church Catches a Whiff of Trouble in the Air," *Evangelical Missions Quarterly*, 32 (April, 1996) 198-204.

[9]David B. Barrett, "Annual Statistical Table on Global Mission: 1997," *International Bulletin of Missionary Research*, 21 (January 1997) 24, 25.

[10]Bob Sjogren and Bill and Amy Stearns, *Run with the Vision* (Minneapolis MN: Bethany House Publishers, 1995) 20-21.

[11]Sjogren, 17.

[12]Barrett (1997).

[13]"Religious Belief Declines in Germany," *The Christian Century*, 29 (January 1997): 94.

[14]George R. Hunsberger and Craig Van Gelder, eds., *The Church Between Gospel and Culture* (Grand Rapids: Eerdmans, 1996).

[15]David J. Hesselgrave, *Today's Choices for Tomorrow's Mission* (Grand Rapids: Zondervan, 1988) 38.

[16]Barrett (1997).

[17]See Marc Spindler, *Bible and Mission: A Partially Annotated Bibliography 1960–1980* (Leiden, Utrecht: Interuniversitair Instituut Voor Missiologie En Oecumenica, 1981).

[18]Karl Barth, *Church Dogmatics*, Vol. 1\2 (Edinburgh: T. & T. Clark, 1956) 280-361.

[19]Don A. Pitman, Ruben L. F. Habit, and Terry C. Muck, *Ministry and Theology in Global Perspective* (Grand Rapids: Eerdmans, 1996).

[20]Pitman, 162ff.

[21]Charles Van Engen, *Mission on the Way* (Grand Rapids: Baker, 1995) 184-217. He evaluates these paradigms and offers his own, an "Evangelistic Paradigm."

[22]Pitman, 223.

[23]Kosuke Koyama, *No Handle on the Cross* (Maryknoll NY: Orbis Books, 1977) 38-39.

[24]Joshua K. Ogawa, "The Benefits and Problems of Internationalizing Missions" in William D. Taylor, ed., *Kingdom Partnerships for Synergy in Missions* (Pasadena CA: William Carey Library, 1994) 173-85.

[25]Ogawa, 174-77.

[26]Valdir Raul Steuernagel, "From Latin America: An Open Letter to the North American Mission Community," in John A. Siewert and John A. Kenyon, eds., *Mission Handbook* (Monrovia CA: Marc, 1993) 47-53.

[27]Jonathan J. Bonk, *Missions and Money* (Maryknoll NY: Orbis Books, 1991).

[28]As quoted in Van Engen, 36.

[29]Lucien Legrand, *Unity and Plurality: Mission in the Bible* (Maryknoll NY: Orbis Books, 1990).

[30]David J. Bosch, *Transforming Mission* (Maryknoll NY: Orbis Books, 1991) 15-178.

[31]Van Engen, 40-43.

[32]Michael J. Anthony, ed., *Short-Term Missions Boom* (Grand Rapids: Baker Books, 1994).

[33]Sjogren, 165-67.

[34]Terry C. Muck, *Alien Gods on American Turf* (Wheaton IL: Victor Books, 1990) and *These Other Religions in Your Neighborhood* (Grand Rapids: Zondervan, 1992).

[35]As quoted in Wilbert R. Shenk, *Write the Vision* (Valley Forge PA: Trinity Press International, 1995) 83.

[36]As quoted in John R. Mott, *The Pastor and Modern Missions* (New York: Student Volunteer Movement for Foreign Missions, 1904) 62.

The Great Commission

Still Relevant for the 21st Century

Russel A. Jones

"Why all the fuss about evangelism?" asked the man as he went out the door shaking his head in disgust.

I had been invited to lead a weekend of evangelistic training sessions for one of our larger churches in Kansas. Since the church was located several hundred miles from the seminary, I made the trip in my "old grubbies" and planned to change before the opening banquet.

When I arrived at the church, I found a restroom and began to change into more appropriate dress. Suddenly the door burst open, and a man came hurrying into the room with some clothes on a hanger. It was evident he had just come from work. He did not seem to notice me at first. He was occupied with trying to untie a knot in the laces of his work shoes. It was only after a groan of irritation when the lace broke that he looked up and noticed me.

"Ha, they got you, too, did they?" Without giving me an opportunity to answer, he continued right on venting his frustration. "I don't see why we have to have these training sessions all the time. I can see you just got off work, too. I had to hurry and get here because my Sunday School class volunteered to be in charge of the serving line. And, if you don't show up, the pastor gets all bent out of shape. So, here is another night shot."

"It might be better than you think," I suggested, hoping to ease his pain a little.

He finished fixing his tie, looked at me very intently, shook his head, and said, "Nope, it won't be. They got some guy from Central Seminary coming to speak to us. It will be so deep, no one will be able to understand it and so dry, you will wonder why you even made the effort to come. Listen, if people want to get saved, there is a church on almost any corner in this city. If they really want to come to God, they will do it on their own. We don't have to spend our time learning to talk them into it. So why all the fuss about evangelism?" With that question, he pushed through the door and disappeared down the hall. For a moment I just stood there looking at the closed door, his remarks still ringing in my ears.

As I went through the food line a few minutes later, he was handing out the buns. When I got to him, he dropped the bun on my plate without the slightest expression of interest. Soon after dinner, the pastor stood and made a lengthy and embellished introduction of the "guy" from the seminary who had come to lead the training sessions. When I came to the podium, I looked over toward the gentleman at the serving table. He took one look at me, rolled his eyes, then turned and walked off into the kitchen. I did not see him again.

It was a humorous incident in one way, but sad in another. His question, "Why all the fuss about evangelism?" made an indelible mark on my heart that evening, and I tried all weekend to answer his question through the presentations I shared with those people who attended the training sessions.

WHY EVANGELIZE?

"Why all the fuss about evangelism?" That question could well be the most important question facing the church of Jesus Christ today. Why should churches hold evangelism training workshops? Why invite special speakers to challenge the membership? Why hold evangelism crusades and revivals? Why all the fuss about evangelism? Haven't we moved beyond this in our modern and progressive world? My answer is: No, we have not.

According to John R. Mott, the supreme purpose for the Christian church and every Christian is: "to make Jesus Christ known, trusted, loved, obeyed, and exemplified in the whole range of individual life—body, mind, and spirit—and also in all human relationships."[1] Christianity is simply the daily expression of the assurance of one's relationship to Christ as seen in his or her relationships. Robert E. Coleman was right when he said,

> Where we begin in evangelism largely determines where we will end. If we begin with the human predicament, there is little to keep us from ending in frustration, if not despair. But, if we start with God, our attention fixed on things above where God reigns in eternal triumph, the vision of God's glory inspires to greater resolve and confidence.[2]

Confidence is a key ingredient in personal evangelism. If we are to exhibit a consistent witness for Christ, we must be confident of our message and our own relationship with Christ.

Michael Green, writing a preface to Max Warren's volume, *I Believe in the Great Commission*, describes contemporary Christianity as having lost its nerve. He states,

> We live in an age where everything is relative, nothing absolute. When nothing is black and white, everything different shades of grey, and to maintain that Christianity is true, that Jesus really is the way to God, and that obedience to Him inevitably carries with it the imperative to mission, is thoroughly unpopular.[3]

He challenges us to learn from the mistakes of the past and recapture the zeal of those early Christians who turned the world upside down.

"Ultimately, the evidence for the credibility of the gospel in the eyes of the world will rest upon the evidence of a quality of life manifested in the church which the world cannot find elsewhere,"[4] wrote William Temple, more than fifty years ago. These words are just as true today as when they were spoken. If men and women are to be reached with the gospel of Christ, they will be reached by committed followers of Christ who have accepted Christ's commission. I agree with Schweer, who wrote that the only way a large number of unsaved people will be reached is through personal evangelism; crusades only reach a portion of the people.[5] W. Stanley Mooneyham also calls for the witness of individual Christians:

> Opportunities await the committed followers of Christ. The need for capable and committed Christians is greater today than at any other time in the history of the church. From every nation and culture, the church needs men and women of faith who have a solid understanding of Scripture who are sensitive to the differences between societies and who can communicate the gospel fully and clearly.[6]

Clearly, if we are to make Christ known to the non-Christian population, witnesses are needed. We need people who will share with others what has happened to them personally in relation to Jesus Christ. Theory is not needed—only facts.[7]

There are several reasons the followers of Jesus Christ should get excited about evangelism and want to tell the good news of salvation. These are all motivating factors for evangelism that can enhance the church's ministry of outreach in the 21st century.

(1) *It is God's will that no one perish.* "The Lord is not slow about his promise, as some think of slowness, but is patient with you, not wanting any

to perish, but all to come to repentance" (2 Pet 3:9). This desire of God is so strong that Jesus revealed it in his own words: "For God so loved the world that he gave his only Son, so that everyone who believes in him may not perish but may have eternal life" (John 3:16). Jesus further underscored this truth by reminding us of the purpose of his mission here on earth: "For the Son of Man came to seek out and to save the lost" (Luke 19:10).

(2) *There will be a judgment.* This is not a popular subject among most people today. Many try to explain it away. Others ignore its truth, while a multitude of men and women hope it is just some story concocted by the church to scare them into the ranks of the religious. Jesus spoke more about judgment than he did about the blessings of heaven. Notice his emphasis of judgment in these words: "God did not send the Son into the world to condemn the world, but in order that the world might be saved through him. Those who believe in him are not condemned; but those who do not believe are condemned already, because they have not believed in the name of the only Son of God" (John 3:17, 18). John the Baptist added to this truth through his testimony of Jesus: "Whoever believes in the Son has eternal life; whoever disobeys the Son will not see life, but must endure God's wrath" (John 3:36). One needs only to read Revelation 20 to see the truth of the judgment as it is revealed in the last days.

(3) *Christ appeals to all.* One of the most thrilling aspects of the gospel of Christ is its universal appeal. Paul tells us, "Everyone who calls on the name of the Lord shall be saved" (Rom 10:13). This universal appeal of the gospel was one of the main strengths of the message received so readily in Russia when I taught at the University of Nizhni Novgorod in 1993. I was asked repeatedly why I was a Christian. Students wanted to know what caused me to become a Christian and learn their language and come to teach them. They listened intently as I shared about the power, the goodness, and the truth of the gospel. But when I spoke of the universal invitation of the gospel, it really caught their attention. They found it hard to believe that anybody and everybody was welcome to come to Christ. They were amazed to learn that the Baptist church was made up of people of all nationalities, economic and social backgrounds, and especially different theological orientations. Their innocent amazement reminded me once again of the uniqueness of the Christian faith. We sometimes get so close to it that we tend to lose its unique perspective.

(4) *Christ commands us to share the good news.* Under the commands of Christ the obligation of evangelism takes root in the human heart. Our Lord has commanded us to share the good news. His words are not options, nor

are they suggestions. They are our marching orders into the 21st century. They are just as valid and applicable today as they were the moment they came from his lips 2,000 years ago. Nowhere in all of Christian literature does it say that they have been rescinded, superseded, or cancelled. The Great Commission is still in effect. Christ's command has not changed. God's method of reaching the world is still the same. Jesus used two important verbs in his vocabulary: "come" and "go." When we accept him as Lord and Savior, we are under obligation to go forth in his name. This command is not a program thought up by a committee or a scheme planned by a group of enthusiastic people.[8]

THE COMMAND

The 21st century is considered by many Christian leaders to be a period of opportunity for the gospel without parallel in human history. The Great Commission will become even more important if the church is to assume its responsibility in the face of such massive social, moral, and economic issues facing the new century. In the words of the famous evangelist Billy Graham:

> We, as God's ambassadors, are called to sound the warning to make judg-ment clear, to call sinners to repentance, to announce God's grace, to direct them to Calvary and the God-man on the cross, to point to the empty tomb, to shout the good news from the housetops, to shout the way of peace with God and peace between (people) and nations.[9]

Wherever the church is authentically Christian, the conviction yet lives that its sole purpose for existence is to proclaim the gospel of the Kingdom of Christ. The commission is still held to be in force, the commission to share the gospel with the world. According to Robert Coleman,

> Herein lies the genius of his strategy to win the world, raising up a holy people who will praise him forever. Disciples, by nature, develop in the likeness of their Lord, and in the process, become participants in his min-istry, thereby reproducing the cycle of growth. By making this the focal concern, Jesus ensures an ever-enlarging working force, ultimately reaching the ends of the earth.[10]

So important was Christ's command to share the gospel that it is recorded no less than five times in the New Testament.

All authority in heaven and on earth has been given to me. Go therefore and make disciples of all nations, baptizing them in the name of the Father and of the Son and of the Holy Spirit, and teaching them to obey everything that I have commanded you. And remember, I am with you always, to the end of the age. (Matt 28:18-20)

Go into all the world and proclaim the good news to the whole creation. The one who believes and is baptized will be saved; but the one who does not believe will be condemned. (Mark 16:15-16)

Thus it is written, that the Messiah is to suffer and to rise from the dead on the third day, and that repentance and forgiveness of sins is to be proclaimed in his name to all nations, beginning from Jerusalem. You are witnesses of these things. And see, I am sending upon you what my Father promised; so stay here in the city until you have been clothed with power from on high. (Luke 24:46-49)

Peace be with you. As the Father has sent me, so I send you. (John 20:21)

[The word translated "sent" according to Warren, is the verbal form of the word apostle. He states, "The witness of the other Gospels shows that this was the underlying conviction of all the teachings of Jesus. He was the apostle of God, sent into the world with a message from God, which message he was."[11] John Stott concludes that the emphasis here on Christ's being sent from the Father makes the mission of Christ our model. In other words, the church's mission comes from our understanding of his mission.[12]]

But you will receive power when the Holy Spirit has come upon you; and you will be my witness in Jerusalem, and in all Judea and Samaria, and to the ends of the earth. (Acts 1:8)

Each of these five commission statements of Christ is important in itself and has enough power and direction in it to be the banner for the church moving into the 21st century. I suggest, however, that we look carefully at the Matthew commission and deal with it as a composite of the others.

THE GREATEST CLAIM

"All authority in heaven and on earth has been given to me." The words of Jesus etch out a blueprint for the Christian church. Without the announcement of his authority, the Great Commission would lack justification and

motivation. But with Christ's authority, his followers can call upon divine power from heaven to direct their ministry and prepare the hearts of the unsaved for the saving message of the gospel.

John Mark Terry seems to capture the essence of this authority in his volume, *Evangelism: A Concise History*. He sums it up quite well:

> The church today could profit from a study of evangelism in the New Testament church. Three things stand out as one examines their work and compares it with modern efforts of evangelism. First, their message was simple. They kept their proclamation so simple that any Christian could share a testimony. Today churches sponsor sixteen-week studies on personal witnessing. These are fine, but witnessing does not have to be that complicated. Second, the early Christians were inspired and guided by the Holy Spirit. The Christians at Jerusalem prayed for ten days and held a one-day crusade. They saw three thousand saved, while many churches today would be delighted with three. Finally, the whole church was active in witnessing. The church today will not grow unless it recovers this emphasis on lay evangelism.[13]

From every nation and culture, the church needs men and women of faith who have a solid understanding of scripture, who are sensitive to the differences between societies, and who can communicate the gospel fully and clearly.

THE GREATEST COMMAND

"Go therefore and make disciples of all nations." The imperative "make disciples" is of utmost importance. This means that witnessing is central, that evangelism is the divine imperative, that sharing the gospel with the unsaved is the very heart of Christ's command to his followers. The New Testament is filled with references to this command.

Jesus' prayer in John 17 is saturated with evangelistic overtones. David Garland observed, "The thrust of his prayer is not that they be saved from harm, but that they remain true to the mission of the one who sent them" (John 17:11, 15, 18, 21).[14] Blauw commented, "They have not been called 'out' of the world but placed 'in' the world and sent 'to' the world."[15] Leavell, writing nearly sixty years ago, caught the essence of Paul's words in 2 Corinthians 5:20 when he stated, "Ambassadors for Christ grossly misrepresent their sovereign if they do not love souls, yearn for souls, plead for souls, and if necessary, even die for souls."[16] Paul had the same compassion that burned in his master's heart when he declared, "Woe to me if I do not proclaim the gospel" (1 Cor 9:16). C. E. Autry confirmed this compassion when he said, "He was not fearful of physical judgment. A consuming fire burned in Paul's heart. He had to preach. If they arrested him, he would preach to the soldiers to whom he was chained. Preaching was not optional for him; he had to do it. Wherever he was, there he preached."[17]

In spite of its imperfections, the church, in every century and every age is responsible for the message of Christ. Whenever the church has been faithful to its task, it has made significant strides forward. In fact, its vitality has been measured by its evangelistic activity. The church as the visible, tangible presence of Christ in the world manifests its presence through its essential functions. Each of these functions takes its form from the person of Christ, and each has an evangelistic dimension.[18] Michael Green reminds us that when the good news was proclaimed in the 1st century, it made a tremendous impact. "In both Jewish and Gentile backgrounds alike, the word was electric. The Christian evangel came like a spark to the tinder of ancient society."[19] A church that ceases to be evangelistic inevitably loses much of its power.

THE GREATEST PICTURE TESTIMONY

"Baptize them in the name of the Father and of the Son and of the Holy Spirit." The Great Commission is clear that we are to make disciples and not just seek out decisions. We are to baptize the converts and bring them into the local church where they can be discipled and begin to grow into Christlikeness. Paul also directs us in his words to the Christians at Colossae: "It is he whom we proclaim, warning everyone and teaching everyone in all wisdom, so that we may present everyone mature in Christ" (Col 1:28).

I have collected numerous definitions of evangelism over the years. Some are quite simple, while others are more complex. The definition that has grasped and held my attention, however, is that of George Sweazey in his excellent work, *The Church as Evangelist*. He seems to capture the very heart of these words of Jesus. He states,

> Evangelism is every possible way of reaching outside the church: To make contacts with definite persons, to cultivate their knowledge of Christian faith and living, to lead them to confess Christ as Lord and Savior, to bring them into church membership, and to help them commence Christian habits and church participation.[20]

I think Sweazey falls a little short of a perfect definition in that he does not make a place for the work of the Holy Spirit. But because of its reflection of the Great Commission, for more than a decade I have used this definition in my evangelism courses. I present it as "Sweazey's Five C's"—contacts, cultivate, confess, church membership, and commence. I also add implied ministry of the Holy Spirit.

THE GREATEST CHALLENGE

"Teach them to obey everything that I have commanded you." The church is responsible for the spiritual welfare of new Christians. They have to be taught the things of Christ. Helping them to become students of the word of God is essential. Assisting them in the establishment of a sound devotional life and giving opportunities for training, ministering, and developing of their spiritual gifts are important parts of the discipling process. Disciplers should assist new Christians in the following tasks:

- knowing what the Bible presents about Christ, why they believe what the Bible presents, and how to confidently offer a witness or testimony concerning those beliefs
- becoming integrated into the local church body and active in its program
- developing consistency and practice at home, school, and work
- becoming deeply and deliberately involved in expressing and living social justice within the church and community
- realizing responsibility to share with others what they have experienced in Christ

Evangelism and discipleship cannot be separated. They are the opposite sides of the same coin. Neither can be carried out effectively without the other. Miles presented the same thought when he stated, "I seriously doubt that one can arrive at a solid biblical foundation for understanding the meaning of evangelism apart from discipleship."[21]

The biggest void in ministry today is the lack of discipleship in the Christian church. All too many new Christians are left to "die on the vine," because more seasoned brothers and sisters in Christ fail to provide training through close association and fellowship. When churches do not make available to new Christians discipleship programs or other forms of help, most of these converts do not grow into providers for others. When there is no follow-up and new Christians do not continue to grow into Christlikeness, the evangelistic ministry of the church is severely hampered, if not cut off completely. The evangelized will not become evangelists unless they are discipled and taught their responsibility under the banner of the Great Commission of Christ.

THE GREATEST PROMISE

"I am with you always, to the end of the age." Jesus has promised in the person of the Holy Spirit to be with us, sustain us, guide us, and direct us, come what may—until the task is finished—even to the end of the age. We are to go into all the world with all the gospel, all the time, in all the power of God, and God will be with us all the way.[22]

Every person who knows Jesus Christ as Savior and acknowledges him as Lord should be a soul winner. It is this promise of Jesus, to be with us, that makes winning souls a reality. Every believer should bear witness to the saving power of Jesus Christ and urge men and women to trust him for their salvation.

No believer should selfishly rest in the spiritual light of the son of righteousness, oblivious to the spiritual needs of others. All believers should put forth some concerted and prayerful effort to reach out to the unreached. Those who name the name of Jesus Christ and claim him as Lord have been given a possession too wonderful and valuable to keep to themselves. Through this precious promise from the Lord to always be with them, they have the power to be what they never thought they could be, do what they never thought they could do, and say what they never thought they could say. The only way this precious promise can ever be fully realized is by the repeated efforts to bring others into the joy of the same salvation.

I think Posterski was right on target when he referred to the followers of Christ as privileged people. He put it this way:

> The followers of Jesus are privileged people. Our life in Christ not only launches us on a journey toward wholeness, our experiences in life fit with God's original design for His creation. Engaging the modern world around us with a credible gospel offers us another privilege. We have the delight of working with God to invite the people who, through our lives, join the journey too.[23]

This engagement is what Barna calls the "bridge" we are to build between our love for God and our love for God's people. As the Holy Spirit works in and through our lives and we share the good news of Christ, God can complete the transformation of a person for God's purposes and glory.[24] This is evangelism in the fullest sense of the word. There is no way around the Great Commission for the Christian—it is imperative.

THE MESSAGE

The second challenge of the Great Commission to the church today is the message it is to share with the world. The message needs to be plain, simple, relevant, and practical. What is this message? The fact that God is the lover of all souls; that our sins have separated us from God; that Jesus Christ has come to pay the price for our sins; and that we need to respond to Christ in faith. These four simple truths are the "warp" of the Christian message, giving it strength and stability.

The problem of communication has always been one with which the church has wrestled. Proclaiming the gospel of Christ in a clear and inviting manner is a task the church of the 21st century must master if it is to be effective in the technological age spreading out before it. I like Duffet's suggestions in his volume on communication within the scope of the church's outreach ministry. He points out:

> Throughout the history of the church, good communications have renewed, revived, and awakened congregations. Technically, churches cannot be renewed or revived; only people can. However, renewed individuals change congregations and denominations and create new ones. In other words, effective communications have always been instrumental in making the Christian faith and church involvement meaningful.[25]

One need only to glance from the attendance board to the pews to know something is wrong in the majority of our churches. Duffet thinks the problem rests squarely on how the gospel message is being communicated from the pulpits. He calls for a change in method.[26]

The problem with the biblical message is not with its content. It is the sure word of God. The way we have "packaged" the message, however, has often created more confusion than it has brought clarity. That in itself has turned many people away from the claims of Christ and has caused many Christians to forsake obedience to the Lord's commission to make disciples.

As we move into the next century with the gospel, I am calling for biblical ethics to become the qualifying factor for the sharing of the gospel message. I define biblical ethics in these words: the biblically inspired rules of conduct and moral obligations that are ours in relation to human and spiritual values as we interact with other persons.

The 21st century will open the door to a more person-to-person orientation. The present computer culture with all its "plug-in" cognates will challenge us to look for people we can trust. We will be drawn to those relatives and friends who seem to know what they believe and why they believe it. A trusting friendship will be the key that will cut across generational lines.

In the 21st century, if we will adhere to this as our guide, we can reduce many liabilities in witnessing. Following are some guidelines that flow from such an approach.

(1) *Adhere to moral integrity.* Since eternal destinies lie in the balance, we will need to be pure and honest in our motives for sharing. We will not abuse the rights and freedoms of our friends and loved ones. We will respect their right to refuse the message if they so desire without our resorting to manipulation or coercion.

Sharing the gospel of Christ with unsaved relatives should be as natural as sharing stories of mutual interest with a good friend. Using the person-oriented approach will afford concerned followers of Christ the natural lines of discussions with their relatives. Building a bridge to relatives and spending the time required to earn a "hearing" about the most significant event in one's life will still be the most effective way to reach unreached relatives.

(2) *Be sensitive.* We will need to become in tune with another's feelings and impressions. We will be sensitive to situations and circumstances surrounding our encounter with an unsaved person. We will realize the possibility that this person may have little or no religious background. We will be kind and gentle in our approach.

Many of our friends and acquaintances are involved in lifestyles that tend to turn us off and cause us to avoid a confrontation, but we must overcome our fear and disgust. These dear ones need the Lord Jesus, and we may be their only hope. Again, the threshold for witness is that of personal interest and concern without a judgmental attitude. In some cases only prayer will open the door for a verbal witness. When that time comes—and it will—we must approach our friends with love, understanding, and patience.

(3) *Be assured of the Spirit's power.* We will take the message of Christ in full assurance of the power of the Holy Spirit. We will realize that forgiveness is possible to everyone, and that no one will be denied the salvation promised by Christ.

Jim was an alcoholic and foul-mouthed neighbor. His language to his wife and children was offensive as well as abusive. Most of the Christians living near Jim had determined him as "hopeless" and had not tried to establish a relationship. His stock expression was, "You only go around the world once, and I am going to ride it for all it's worth." He was an executive with a six-figure income. He had cars, a boat, and a summer cottage. He seemed to, as he put it, "have the world by the tail." After much prayer, I decided to approach Jim at his point of interest—cars. He responded immediately to my question about setting spark plug gaps. He brought his tools over and helped me do some minor repairs. It was from this simple show of interest in Jim that our friendship began to grow and is still growing. He now talks openly with me about religious things and makes apology when he "slips" in his language.

(4) *Be accountable.* We will witness to the saving power of Christ in full realization of the privilege we have to bear the good news of Christ. We will remember that we are responsible to share the message in a plain and simple manner. Above all, we will remember that as children of God we are ultimately accountable to God.

Many people sit in the ashes of their "burned-out" dreams and feel there is no hope. Sometimes we, too, feel that way when we observe the circumstances of some persons around us. But we are accountable to our God. We are under obligation to share the good news of Jesus Christ and seek to make disciples of all people. The Bible tells us that no one is beyond the saving love of Christ. This simple fact must become the driving force that keeps us faithful to our commission. We must seek ways to build bridges to others regardless of their circumstances. We need to pray for the Lord to open their hearts to our interest and concern. Beginning where persons are, we must seek to assist them to move toward a salvation experience and a continual growth into Christlikeness.

CONCLUSION

The Great Commission is still valid for the local church moving into the 21st century. It will always be the marching orders for the church. The church stands today between the coming of the Holy Spirit at Pentecost and the second coming of Jesus Christ. The church's major responsibility is to be faithful to its Lord's commission to make his saving grace known in all its fullness and power throughout the earth.[27]

Warren reminds us that moving into the 21st century is much like the position of the world as it stood on the threshold of history prior to World War II. Our study of history paints a bleak picture of those earlier years as

Hitler was emerging and Europe was thrown into chaos. The future was unclear, unsettled, and hopeless to most Europeans.

This same attitude seems to cloud much of our world today. Dictators and war have been replaced by the technical revolution with all of its ramifications. Much of life seems so impersonal, distant, and detached. Many people are retreating into the isolation of individualism where there is little room to show concern for others, especially in relation to the claims of Jesus Christ. This is a reflection of the man who came to the church in Kansas for the training event but really did not see any value in being there.

Warren closes his excellent volume on the Great Commission with an excerpt from the martyred Martin Niemoller's message to the German Christians concerning their responsibility to the Great Commission in 1933 with these words:

> "We have nothing to produce, nothing with which to appease the hunger of the multitude . . . so that it may be visible to all eyes that we Christians are nothing ourselves; that we Christians do nothing ourselves. We live by a miracle, and this miracle is called Christ: he is everything; he has everything; he does everything."

> That is the testimony that we as Christians owe to those who today come to us with their hopes and problems and expectations. We are not concerned with the question of how these crowds of unsettled men and women stand with regard to Christianity and the Christian Church; our duty is to see that these men and women meet the miracle called Christ.[28]

Roland Leavell labels the Great Commission as the "Magna Carta" of evangelism.[29] True, it is timeless in its authority and binding on its recipients. May we bow before our Lord and Savior with the humility and commitment of Samuel and say with our whole heart, "Speak Lord, your servants are listening." Amen.

NOTES

[1]John R. Mott, *The Larger Evangelism* (New York: Abingdon-Cokesbury Press, 1944) 7.

[2]Robert E. Coleman, "The Affirmation of the Great Commission," *Journal of the Academy for Evangelism in Theological Education* (Nashville, 1990-1991)6:32.

[3]Michael Green, "Editor's Preface," *I Believe in the Great Commission*, by Max Warren (Grand Rapids: Eerdmans, 1976) iii.

[4]William Temple, *Towards the Conversion of England* (London: The Press and Publications Board of the Church Assembly, 1943) 121.

[5]G. William Schweer, *Personal Evangelism for Today* (Nashville: Broadman Press, 1984) 27.

[6]W. Stanley Mooneyham, "Foreword" to David M. Howard's *The Great Commission for Today* (Downers Grove IL: InterVarsity Press, 1976) vii.

[7]Russel A. Jones, *Victorious Christian Living* (Valley Forge PA: Judson Press, 1983) 49.

[8]Billy Graham, *A Biblical Standard for Evangelists* (Minneapolis MN: World Wide Publications, 1984) 27.

[9]Ibid, 28.

[10]Robert E. Coleman, ed., *Evangelism: On the Cutting Edge* (Old Tappen NJ: Power Books, Fleming H. Revell, 1986) 129.

[11]Max Warren, *I Believe in the Great Commission* (Grand Rapids: Eerdmans, 1976) 172.

[12]John R. W. Stott, *Christian Mission in the Modern World* (Downers Grove IL: InterVarsity Press, 1975) 23.

[13]John Mark Terry, *Evangelism: A Concise History* (Nashville: Broadman and Holman, 1994) 27.

[14]David E. Garland, "Evangelism in the New Testament," *Review and Expositor* (Louisville KY: Southern Baptist Theological Seminary, Fall 1980) 464.

[15]Ibid.

[16]Roland Q. Leavell, *Evangelism: Christ's Imperative Commission* (Nashville: Broadman Press, 1951) 6.

[17]C. E. Autrey, *Basic Evangelism* (Grand Rapids: Zondervan, 1959) 34.

[18]Ben Campbell Johnson, *Rethinking Evangelism: A Theological Approach* (Philadelphia: Westminster, 1987) 80.

[19]Michael Green, *Evangelism in the Early Church* (Grand Rapids: Eerdmans, 1970) 57.

[20]George E. Sweazey, *The Church as Evangelist* (New York: Harper and Row, 1978) 53.

[21]Delos Miles, *Introduction to Evangelism* (Nashville: Broadman Press, 1983) 22.

[22]Charles L. Chaney and Granville Watson, *Evangelism: Today and Tomorrow* (Nashville: Broadman Press, 1993) 28.

[23]Donald C. Posterski, *Reinventing Evangelism* (Downers Grove IL: InterVarsity Press, 1989) 172

[24]George Barna, *Evangelism That Works* (Ventura CA: Gospel Light Publishers, 1995) 27.

[25]Robert G. Duffett, *A Relevant Word* (Valley Forge PA: Judson Press, 1995) xiii.

[26]Ibid.

[27]David M. Howard, *The Great Commission for Today* (Downers Grove IL: InterVarsity Press, 1976) 105.

[28]Warren, 183.

[29]Leavell, 3.

THE NEW TESTAMENT

HOW WILL WE INTERPRET IT FOR THE 21ST CENTURY?

David May

David May [signature]

EVERYONE IS AN INTERPRETER OF THE NEW TESTAMENT. Attempting to understand what the New Testament means is not the domain of any single denomination, church, biblical scholar, or TV evangelist. Even though some might attempt to establish and distribute the "authoritative" interpretation of a biblical passage, the fact still remains that everyone who picks up a Bible and reads the New Testament is a potential interpreter.

The reason for proliferation of New Testament interpreters is because most individuals in the United States (97%) can read. Couple this fact with the availability of the New Testament in English or almost any other language, and this allows everyone to express his or her "interpretation." A person can claim to know what Jesus really meant when he said, "There are eunuchs who have been made eunuchs by others, and there are eunuchs who have made themselves eunuchs for the sake of the kingdom of heaven. Let anyone accept this who can" (Matt 19:12). One might claim to know exactly what Paul meant when he said, "As in all the churches of the saints, women should be silent in the churches. For they are not permitted to speak, but should be subordinate" (1 Cor 14:33b-34). Then there are individuals who believe they have the interpretative wisdom to decipher "the number of the beast, for it is the number of a person. Its number is six hundred sixty-six" (Rev 13:18).

Everyone may not realize that they are biblical interpreters, but by statements such as "I think . . .," "It seems to me . . .," or "I believe . . . ," individuals are engaging in giving their interpretations (perceptions) on biblical passages. Even those who sense that New Testament interpretation is beyond their grasp will still find "professional" interpretations with which they resonate and will appeal for support to an authoritative book, pastor, or teacher. No one has a monopoly on interpreting Scripture today.

John and Joanna Q. Public as interpreters of Scripture is a phenomenon that has Baptist roots. Martin E. Marty, a church historian and an astute observer of society and religion, has said that a process of "baptification" is now happening in American religion. He means that certain baptistic beliefs and practices are finding their way into acceptance in different American religious traditions. This is certainly true when it comes to understanding Scripture. The Baptist belief espoused by E. Y. Mullins, "The right of private judgment as to the meaning of the Bible is of course another aspect of the [soul's competency],"[1] is being practiced by everyone. While some people are better interpreters than others, at the most basic level, everyone is an interpreter.

Not only is everyone an interpreter of the New Testament, but this attempt to understand the New Testament is an action that takes place everyday and everywhere. The interpretation of Scripture is not an event restricted just to Sundays or the context of church and synagogue. People are engaged in discussing and interpreting the Bible in all kinds of places. A person can overhear spontaneous interpretations taking place between women on a softball field, men shopping in grocery stores, or students at a seminary. One can also find organized Bible study groups springing up wherever people gather. These groups meet daily, weekly, or monthly. The slogan used to be that "the sun never sets on the British Empire"; today it could be rephrased as "the sun never sets on biblical interpreters." Around the globe at this very minute, someone is reading (misreading?) and interpreting (misinterpreting?) the New Testament.

The use of computers has accelerated interpretation also within national and global settings. While TV and radio only allowed for one-way interpretation, usually by way of the currently popular evangelist or trend, now with E-mail and chatlines a person can experience interactive interpretation. And perhaps because of the anonymity, an individual may be even bolder in expressing a particular interpretative view than he or she would in person. The World Wide Web is filled with interpretations and interpreters of biblical passages that are only a click away. The interpretation range of material on the Internet ranges from the boring to the bizarre.

This explosion of biblical interpretation should cause people to rejoice. Or should it? Yes, the Bible is being read and studied, but is the word of God being "rightly handled" (2 Tim 2:15)? Even a random sampling of interpretations on one passage will demonstrate a wide range of differing views. These interpretations are not only different, but many stand in tension with each other. Individuals use their varied interpretations as warrants or validations for all types of agendas. Perhaps all of this should give us a reflective pause before applauding interpreting by everyone, everywhere, and all the time.

When I was teaching tennis, I used a simple, and not scientifically gathered, statistic to teach my tennis students the difference between tennis players and *tennis players*. I used to say that 97% of people *play at* tennis while only 3% *play* tennis. In observing those who interpret the New Testament, I have reached a similar conclusion. It seems that 97% of New Testament readers *play at* interpreting, while only 3% *truly interpret*. Now this might raise some religious hackles from those who feel I am not being fair to that earnest Christian in Spikard, Missouri, who is reading the New Testament. I do believe there are sincere Christians reading the Bible and generating meaning from their readings. However, one needs to acknowledge that sincerity does not always equal good interpretation. The Branch Davidians in Waco, Texas, should be an example in recent memory to put that belief to rest.

The central question, therefore, is not: will we interpret Scripture? Of course, we will. And the question is not: when and where we will interpret? We will interpret the New Testament at all times and everywhere. The central question today is: *how* will we interpret the New Testament? The how question will become more crucial in the 21st century because of continuing and escalating clashes between competing interpretative viewpoints, especially related to hot-button social issues. A humorous satire written by Erasmus more than 400 years ago anticipates the types of conflicts we will continue to see. In this satire, Polymeus has been in a dispute with a man about defending the gospel and tells a friend how he dealt with the conflict:

> I met the man privately, grabbed him by the hair with my left hand, and punched him with my right. I gave him a hell of a beating; made his whole face swell. What do you say to that? Isn't that promoting the Gospel? Next I gave him absolution by banging him on the head three times with this very same book [New Testament] raising three lumps, in the name of the Father, Son, and Holy Ghost.[2]

The how question is also important because there is growing cynicism about any and all understandings of the New Testament. Individuals are perhaps skeptical that there is any certainty when it comes to a particular interpretation on a specific passage. As Perry Yoder observed,

> With so many different interpretational games being played, it is not surprising that people often become suspicious of the validity of any interpretation. Interpretation for many comes close to being a synonym for opinion, as in the expression "Well, that's your interpretation." In such a

state of affairs, interpretations are chosen on the basis of one's own opinion. If the result of someone else's study agrees with us, then it must be right; if it doesn't, we feel free to reject it.[3]

BAGGAGE WE ARE LUGGING INTO THE 21ST CENTURY

When the clock strikes 12:00 A.M. on January 2000 (or is it 2001?), we will not leave behind all the baggage of the 20th century. I don't expect to wake up and have a new perspective on velvet Elvis portraits, the taste of brussels sprouts, or rap music. Several trends for how people have interpreted the New Testament in the past will be carried forward into the 21st century, and these need to be acknowledged if we want to cultivate better ways to be good interpreters for the 21st century.

WHAT YOU SEE IS WHAT YOU GET
—LITERALISM

This way of interpreting the New Testament is easy, simple, and attempted by many. It is simply the form of interpreting that equates reading with meaning; what you see is what you get. This approach gives the interpreter the satisfaction of saying that he or she takes the Bible literally because he or she accepts "what the Bible says, and what it clearly means." This flat reading of the New Testament can have the most disastrous effects. In my grandmother's hometown, there was a man who used this simplistic style of interpretation. He read the passage where Jesus said, "If your hand offends you, cut it off." And he did. My grandmother, who interpreted her own Bible with a what-you-see-is-what-you-get approach, said, "I don't think he was reading the Bible right on this point." I said to her "Bingo, you're right."

A what-you-see-is-what-you-get approach causes one to miss the differences in the forms of writing that make up the New Testament. The New Testament is a collection of letters, gospels, an apocalypse and an acts. Within these forms are other forms such as parables, healing and exorcism stories, lists, and numerous symbols. To read every form as the same, literally, is like reading the letters one receives in the daily mail the same, whether it is the gas bill or the "you may already be a winner" letter.

This approach can breed a false type of pietism built on the sandy soil of "I take the Bible literally." It also has the potential to paint other interpreters of the Scripture as less than good interpreters and at worst as suspect Christians. Yoder points out the fallacy of such an approach that "hides what is really happening. In reality, what is presented as the 'literal meaning' is the interpretation chosen by the person himself [herself], not the meaning that the passage must have."[4]

IT DOESN'T MEAN WHAT IT SEEMS
—SPIRITUALIZING AND ALLEGORY

I remember when growing up being fascinated by biblical interpreters who could take one little passage and begin wringing all kinds of meaning out of it. At the end of these sermons or Bible study gymnastics, I thought with admiration, "Gee, I had never seen all that in that passage before." Actually, it was never there. In contrast to taking the Scriptures at face value, this way of reading says that an interpreter pries up the crusty old story and looks underneath for the fresh hidden meaning. This is usually done by way of allegorizing and spiritualizing. An interpreter who uses allegory sees every element within a passage as representing something beyond itself. The surface meaning is only a husk; the truth lurks within and needs only for a creative interpreter to unleash it. This trend will be carried into the 21st century because it has been around since the 2nd century. The church leader Augustine of Hippo (345–430 A.D.) is an example of an interpreter in the past who practiced this way of interpreting. His reading of the parable of the Good Samaritan (Luke 10:29-37) is a classical example:

> *A certain man went down from Jerusalem to Jericho;* Adam himself is meant; *Jerusalem* is the heavenly city of peace, from whose blessedness Adam fell; *Jericho* means the moon, and signifies our mortality, because it is born, waxes, wanes, and dies. *Thieves* are the devil and his angels. *Who stripped him,* namely, of his immortality; *and beat him,* by persuading him to *sin; and left him half-dead,* because in so far as man can understand and know God, he lives, but in so far as he is wasted and oppressed by sin, he is dead; he therefore is called *half-dead.*[5]

This is enough of an example to see the extreme form that allegories can take when it comes to finding the hidden meaning in Scripture. Allegories only display that an interpreter already has a viewpoint he or she reads into the scripture passage.

While the above example is complex and detailed, most 20th-century interpreters are not usually so extravagant in their detailing of New Testament passages. They practice a more restrained form of interpretation I call "spiritualizing." The goal of spiritualizing is to make New Testament passages understandable and acceptable for 21st-century interpreters. It is a quest to be relevant for modern people. In the process, however, unlikely analogies are made, and the radical edge of the original story is often dulled. For example, consider the story about Paul being led away to Rome in chains as found in the Acts of the Apostles. In spiritualizing this story, some interpreters could say that we all have chains that bind us—alcohol, sex, money, etc.—and we are all being led to judgment. Or consider the example of the storm in which the disciples find themselves in Mark 4. According to a spiritualizing approach, we often find ourselves in the storms of life. Storm becomes a metaphor for anything happening in one's life that is disruptive or tumultuous. The conclusion is usually that in these storms of life, only Jesus brings calm.[6]

SKEWING THE VIEW
—INTERPRETING BY OUR EXPERIENCES

One interpretative trend of the 20th century that will be carried into the 21st century is reading the New Testament through our personal experience. This approach is good and bad. On the positive side, we are asked to bring ourselves to the New Testament. To bring all that we are as fallible human beings to the revelation of God is an awe-stirring event. When it happens well, it can allow us to hear our story in the biblical story, and that hearing can shape us.[7] If we do not attempt to hear our story in the pages of the Bible, then it becomes just an ancient story that has little impact on our lives.

   The continuing interest in spirituality and the integration of the self with a spiritual dimension will continue the trend toward very personalized readings. In such readings, individuals interpret the New Testament from their personal experience, such as, a woman, an African-American, a Hispanic, a white southern male, and on and on. However, in trying to find ways to make the New Testament story our story, and in reading all the passages of the New Testament through our personal and privatized lens, we may construct meanings that are very idiosyncratic. For this reason, Richard Hays' point is well taken: "When we read scripture through the hermeneutic of trust in God, we discover that we should indeed be suspicious—suspicious first of ourselves, because our own minds have been corrupted and shaped by the present evil age."[8]

Often when using one's personal experience as a grid for reading a New Testament passage, one may not even be aware of the baggage one brings to the passage. In other words, reading biblical passages through our personal social and cultural settings will skew the view of reading the New Testament. Children are unabashedly interpreters who use their experiences to interpret Scripture. Recently, a woman working with inner-city children shared with me this telling interpretative experience. She was teaching a group about Jesus instructing his disciples to be "fishers of men." A small boy raised his hand and asked, "Was Jesus gay?" For this child, through his reading lens of the inner city, a man who was fishing for other men had to be gay.

One can be shocked at this child's early interpretative attempt, but it represents what happens all the time with all interpreters. While we may be more sophisticated because of our experiences and in presenting a front that we are objective interpreters, we still follow the childish example of using what we know best—our experiences. Individuals use these experiences as the filter by which to understand events, people, words, and scenarios in the New Testament. In doing so, we impose upon New Testament passages meanings that are relevant for our social settings, agendas, and situations, but may be totally undiscernible for the first readers of the New Testament.[9]

OVER A BILLION INTERPRETATIONS SERVED
—MCINTERPRETERS

There is a 20th-century mentality related to time that will continue into the 21st century and probably will become more predominant. We, especially Westerners, do not like to wait; we do not like to "waste" time. Spending time stalled in traffic leads to a phenomenon called "road rage." VCRs allows us to fast forward over pesky commercials. Computer microprocessors operate at speeds faster than we can click and input. And of course, the paradigm of fastness for our society is McDonald's. A lunch meal that used to take a person in the 1920s an hour to prepare, cook, and eat can now be cooked, flipped, mayo-swabbed, packed, and delivered to you in a matter of minutes. With such forces at work upon us, we may have a tendency to become "McInterpreters." We want our interpretations fast, neat, and nicely served.

When someone asks the question, "What does this passage mean?" and an answer goes into the context, history, and other complex issues, he or she risks glazed eyes and a nodding head. Plodding, reading, researching, and rereading do not seem to be part of the makeup for current interpreters. Yet, ironically, individuals will spend hours researching in *Consumer Report* to find the best toaster, sunscreen, or tires, but will spend virtually no time at the interpretation of Scripture. Because great amounts of time are needed for working out an interpretation, and this time is not always spent, two things are likely to happen for contemporary interpreters.

First is the nondiscriminative use of authorities who have pre-packaged New Testament interpretations. There can be a tendency to accept these interpretations because they are the latest craze in understanding a passage of Scripture. On the other hand, one may reject something that is new without even considering it. Either approach toward interpretations is unhealthy.

Another nondiscriminating tendency among student interpreters is that they will go to the library shelves and pull off the oldest book on a Scripture passage. Without discriminating about the authority, they believe that the oldest sources must be the most authoritative. I always ask these interpreters one question: "If you had to have major surgery, would you want your physician to be trained by an 1880-volume of medicine?" They always say they would want her to have the latest and most up-to-date reading. Wise choice.

A second outcome of wanting quick interpretations is that many individuals may select an interpretation because they are overwhelmed by interpreters who dazzle with form even if they have poor or misleading content. Marketing is big business not only in cars, but also in interpretations. This marketing can be seen in the variety of "study" Bibles and study aids available in Christian bookstores. It is also evident in radio, television, and now computer personalities pushing interpretations. In a conference attended by biblical academicians from around the nation, Rev. Jesse Jackson spoke and put his finger on the difference between form and content: "I am with some of the finest minds in the academic world, and yet you are not getting your message out. You have Rolls-Royce brains and bicycle egos. Those on television are the ones with Rolls-Royce egos and bicycle brains."[10]

The fascination with form over content leads to finding simplistic interpretations for passages. The simplistic approach is seen in a bumper-sticker approach that gives a pithy saying that is memorable and used to answer complex issues. Another place is the T-shirt theology, which presents brief interpretative slogans. Between T-shirts, bumper stickers, and sound bites, individuals have, perhaps unconsciously, used too simplistic a foundation for interpreting the larger issues in the New Testament. These interpretative slogans, which unreflective readers of the New Testament cite, usually represent an "authoritative source" with which one already agrees.

How to Interpret for the 21st Century

Being forewarned will help to avoid carrying these interpretative trends into the 21st century. Nothing could be worse in the proliferation of interpretations than to have a greater number of poor interpretations based upon weak methods from the past. However, the question still remains: how will we "rightly handle" the word of God as we carry our New Testaments into the 21st century?

As we enter the 21st century, we have to frequently and loudly remind ourselves that *the 1st century and the 21st century are not alike.* While this seems like a common sense dictum, it is rarely taken to heart. Potential interpreters of the New Testament such as ourselves must acknowledge that there is an incredibly great gulf between the world of the Bible and the contemporary world in which we live, and that to bridge these two worlds is difficult.

The gulf between the biblical world and our present world exists for numerous reasons. At the most basic level of separation, we are distanced by time, almost two thousand years. *Time* is perhaps the most difficult gulf to bridge since time machines exist only in the realm of science fiction. We are separated by the very *language* in which the New Testament was written. Few interpreters of the New Testament know Greek, but it is the language in which God chose to communicate divine revelation to humanity. Does this make a difference? Certainly. No English translation can convey the same meaning as that contained in the Greek. We are separated by *geography.* Unless you are reading this chapter while living in Israel or Western Turkey, you are separated from the places that were so intimately connected with the words of the New Testament. We are separated by *culture*, which perhaps is the most difficult distance to overcome. It is tempting, because it is easy, to read our cultural definitions into the ancient Mediterranean culture of the New Testament. We must avoid the Arrogant Interpreter Club whose motto is: "Since we do it this way, all people of all times must have done it this way."[11]

Because of these distances, a key principle for a 21st century interpreter is to *hear the New Testament passage as the 1st-century reader heard the passage.* A modern saying is that we should not criticize a person until we have walked in his or her shoes. It could be rephrased that we should not interpret a New Testament passage until we have walked in the sandals of those first listeners. What would they have experienced and felt when they heard the words of Jesus or Paul read to them?

A New Testament scholar, Bruce Malina, bluntly stated the importance of first hearing like the original audience when he said, "Ordinary readings produced with no thought to being considerate of what the authors of the [New Testament] said and meant in their original time, place, and culture are, as a rule, unethical reading."[12] This is a rather harsh indictment for many of us who love to read the New Testament and find comfort and meaning in it. However, it does call upon contemporary interpreters to be considerate of their 1st-century ancestors in faith. It is a call not to violate what those original listeners/readers would have understood as the meaning for their day.

Being considerate readers/interpreters places a great responsibility upon any person who takes upon himself or herself the mantle of interpreter. As Malina said, "To be fair to the biblical authors and the persons they refer to, one must make some effort to learn about their culture and the social forms realized through their language."[13] The operative word is to learn. Sometimes in the Christian tradition we acknowledge Jesus as Savior and the salvation that is offered, but we neglect that he is also teacher and our role is as learner. In many of the Gospel stories, particularly John, Jesus is described as teacher. Accepting Jesus as teacher in relationship to interpretation is totally different than accepting him as savior. We love to have Jesus as savior and to have him pull us out of the fire. But teacher? To accept Jesus as teacher is to have more responsibility; it is a call to accountability. Therefore another important element for interpreting in the 21st century is to *learn Jesus' world and words.*

By learning the world and words of Jesus, a person learns about the values, norms, history, and context that made the ancient biblical world. One is called to be a historian, anthropologist, sociologist, literary critic, and linguist. The great gulf between the "then" of the 1st century and the "now" of the coming 21st century can be partially spanned by the construction of a framework built upon knowing the world and values of the first group to whom the New Testament was addressed.

If you have followed the reading of this chapter so far, you are probably wailing, "How can anyone really read and understand the Bible today? It seems like it is only for the professional interpreter or a seminary professor." A biblical story illustrates that this is not a new situation, but one that is as old as the New Testament. In the story of the Ethiopian eunuch and Philip, the Ethiopian is reading the prophet Isaiah when the Spirit compels Philip to ask him, "Do you understand what you are reading?" The Ethiopian's response is, "How can I, unless someone guides me?" Understanding of Scripture is not innate but learned. One has to learn background, history, and literature in order to interpret; and this means time, skills, and sometimes a competent guide.

There will continue to be *a need for professional guides in the interpretation of the New Testament,* those individuals who devote time and energy to interpretation. Just as specialization is a part of most areas in society today, so will it be in the New Testament. Those who specialize in interpretation will assist the rest of us. This situation is not new; the Jewish tradition of interpretation follows this method with skilled interpreters such as priests, judges, elders, prophets, and rabbis.[14]

The responsibility for learning falls heavily upon ministers, preachers, and chaplains as they become skilled interpreters. In the 21st century, these individuals will still represent the front lines of interpretations for thousands of people. The ideas and viewpoints shaped (or misshaped) by this group will influence many. If one is not honest and helpful in interpretation, and if one continues to perpetuate old and simplistic views, one will have a generation of biblical illiterates. And we will be faced with the challenging question a former student of mine asked after class: "Why were we never taught this in church?"

For many of us, another principle to acknowledge is that *we are amateurs at New Testament interpretation.* Amateur is a perfect description for interpreters; it comes from a French term meaning "lovers of." We are lovers of interpretation. We love the New Testament; we want to gain insight from it because we know it to be God's revelation to us. But being "lovers of interpretation" does not mean that we are skilled in interpretation. Our interpretations will not be of the same quality as someone who has researched and studied on a different level. Does this breed despair that the average person cannot interpret on his or her own? Absolutely not! In fact, it is now easier than ever because of the resources available.

An abundance of journals and books exists for help in navigating the terrain of the New Testament, but one must read with a critical eye. Not all books and articles are created equal. Plus, with the computer and Internet, one has the potential to have knowledge for interpreting the Bible at any interpreter's fingertips. For example, in the area of medicine, I am not an expert. If an illness cannot be treated with an aspirin or bandage, then I am lost. However, there now exists on the Internet an incredible array of information related to getting a second opinion about an illness. On June 26, 1997, the National Library of Medicine went on-line with MedLine.[15] It is a database of more than 8.8 million references to articles published in 3,800 biomedical journals. Anyone can access this information for free, if they have a computer.

The 21st century hopefully holds the same type of depository of articles and information for those wanting to interpret the New Testament. In fact, there are many sites already on the Internet where such information can be found. Unfortunately, the quality of much of it is of a dubious nature. Now who will use a resource such as MedLine? People who are serious about what ails them. And who would use NTNet (It doesn't exist, so don't try and access it)? People serious about understanding the New Testament. If such a scenario as NTNet happens, a whole series of questions will arise about access, authorship, oversight, and many others issues. But for now, it is certainly possible that the computer and Internet could serve as valuable resources, especially for individuals (lay and clergy) who do not have access to theological libraries and the expert guides in the field of New Testament.

Another characteristic that must mark interpretation for the 21st century is *the input from community and validation from the community*. The privatization of interpretation must give way to a more community-oriented approach. Willard Swartley, writing on the art of interpretation, said:

> Biblical interpretation is not a private enterprise. In the last analysis it is not the domain of either the individual or the scholar. Interpretation should be tested and validated by communities of faith. The insights and truth claims of one community should be shared with and tested by other communities of faith.[16]

While the privatization of interpretation will continue to be a part of the 21st century, interpreters will have to overcome this strong pull. The view of a lone minister, such as Jonathan Edwards or Elizabeth Cady Stanton, bent over a desk preparing sermons or studies in the isolation of his or her study should be a thing of the past. Community means collaboration in understanding the New Testament and any interpretation of it.

Ironically, a community approach to interpretation has its roots in the 1st-century world and early Jewish tradition of interpretation. The ancient world was a group-oriented world. Scripture was studied in the context of community, and issues of interpretation were debated within the community. The great gathering places, the synagogues, became those community places of interpretation. Jesus' calling of disciples was not only a missionary-oriented group, but also an interpretative community. It was a community that Jesus often challenged to understand his parables, a community he instructed (Mark 4).

Of course, interpreting within a community context does not guarantee that interpretations will be perfect. Some communities are so composed of like-minded individuals, they are simply mutual affirmation societies. Some communities only share individual opinions without integrating groundwork study first. In the New Testament period, the Pharisees are examples of how communities do not always guarantee interpretative integrity. Within the Pharisees, for example, there were differing schools of thought on such issues as to whether or not one can eat an egg laid on the Sabbath. This interpretative debate missed the point of keeping the Sabbath Holy. It took another interpreter from outside, Jesus, to point this out to the group.

When the community of the interpreter operates at its best, it invites new ideas and yet also allows for boundaries. At its best also, it allows for interpretations to be tested and validated.[17] Without the control of a community, an understanding of Scripture can go spinning into the space of endless and strange interpretations. With a community, one can validate an interpretation within the context of the immediate group and also within the history and tradition of the larger Christian community.

CONCLUSION

How will we interpret the New Testament for the 21st century? Partially, we will understand the New Testament like we did in the 20th century. But hopefully, we will learn from the past and, with a greater sense of responsibility for the Word of God, approach the task of interpretation with renewed vigor. In the process we may discover a more lively and radical gospel and a fresher faith. William M. Swartley has characterized the task of how we interpret in this way:

> The Scripture speaks to us only if we are open to its message. . . . Through faithful response to the Word, we discover the power of the biblical message to upbuild the interpreting community—"to break and to heal, to wound and to cure."[18]

Perhaps the prayer that needs to be uttered as we attempt to understand the New Testament is one voiced by the 3rd-century interpreter Origen (182–254?). With a vision that could see into the needs of the 21st century, he voiced this prayer for how we read Scripture:

Lord God, let us keep your Scriptures in mind and meditate on them day and night, persevering in prayer, always on watch. We beg you, Lord, to give us real knowledge of what we read and to show us not only how to understand it, but how to put it into practice, so that we may deserve to obtain spiritual grace, enlightened by the law of the Holy Spirit, through Jesus Christ our Lord, whose power and glory will endure throughout all ages. Amen.

NOTES

[1]E. Y. Mullins, *The Axioms of Religion: A New Interpretation of the Baptist Faith* (Philadelphia: Griffith & Rowland Press, 1908) 56.

[2]Desiderius Erasmus, *The Gospel Bearer* (1529).

[3]Perry B. Yoder, *Toward Understanding the Bible* (Newton KS: Faith and Life Press, 1978) 6.

[4]Ibid., 5.

[5]Augustine, *Quaestiones Evangeliorum*, II, 19.

[6]Sidney Greidanus, *The Modern Preacher and the Ancient Text: Interpreting and Preaching Biblical Literature* (Grand Rapids: Eerdmans, 1988) 160.

[7]Willard M. Swartley, *Slavery, Sabbath, War, & Women: Case Issues in Biblical Interpretation* (Scottsdale PA: Herald Press, 1983) 22.

[8]Richard B. Hays, "Salvation by Trust? Reading the Bible Faithfully," *The Christian Century* (26 February 1997): 221.

[9]David M. May, " 'Drawn from Nature or Common Life': Social and Cultural Reading Strategies for the Parables," 94 *Review & Expositor* (1997): 201.

[10]Jesse Jackson, "Plenary Address," Annual Society of Biblical Literature and American Academy of Religion Meetings, Atlanta GA, November 1986.

[11]Bruce Malina, *The New Testament World: Insights from Cultural Anthropology*, rev. ed. (Louisville KY: Westminster/John Knox, 1993) 11.

[12]Bruce Malina, "The Bible, Witness or Warrant: Reflections on Daniel Patte's *Ethics of Biblical Interpretation*," *Biblical Theology Bulletin* 26 (1996): 84.

[13]Bruce Malina, "Reading Theory Perspective: Reading Luke-Acts," in *The Social World of Luke-Acts: Models for Interpretation*, ed. Jerome Neyrey (Peabody MA: Hendrickson, 1991) 9-10.

[14]James L. Kugel and Rowan A. Greer, *Early Biblical Interpretation* (Philadelphia: Westminster, 1986) 52.

[15]Http://www.nlm.nih.gov/

[16]Swartley, *Sabbath*, 234.

[17]Ibid.

[18]Ibid., 242.

Multiple Interpretations
of the Biblical Text
Why the Church Must Listen

Judith A. Todd

WHY SHOULD THE CHURCH LISTEN to the multiple interpretations of the biblical text? I believe the way our churches answer this question will be crucial to the configuration of denominations in the 21st century. When one interpretation of the Bible dominates the Christian community, it becomes *the* lens through which Christians are to understand the biblical message. Instead of gaining the truth of God's Word, the church limits Christians' ability to hear God speak. When we are able to listen to many interpretations, even though some of them challenge us, we are able to grow in our faith. Dynamic growth enables us to hear and pay attention to God's call for the church to be the agent of the Good News in the midst of a world that is hungry for the saving message of Jesus Christ.

The Bible itself speaks with many voices. Written down over a millennia, the community of faith listened and spoke of God's activities and call in and for new situations. In the millennia since the canon of Scriptures was closed, the church has done its missionary work well. The worldwide Christian church now speaks with many voices and in many languages. In our own day God is calling the church to something new, and our evangelistic efforts need to be refocused in response to God's call.

Thus, we need to listen to multiple interpretations of the biblical text. By listening, we will hear the many voices in the Bible itself; we will learn to trust the voices of Christians around the world; and we will learn not to be afraid of God's call for the church to be the agent of mission in a broken, hurting, secular, hungry, damaged, and damaging world.

Why Question Multiple Interpretations?

Daniel Weiss, General Secretary of the American Baptist Churches USA, spoke at the 1997 Biennial meeting about Christians' need to know the truth of God's Word now more than ever. To know the Word requires interpreting the Word. We depend upon the Holy Spirit to illuminate the Scriptures we read, and, we must confess, we are finite, imperfect people who may hear imperfectly. Weiss explains his experiences in this way:

> I hear from people who are convinced there is only one way to interpret Scripture. Ordinarily, it is their way. How, then, do we account for different denominations and theologies? Why do we ever have differences of opinion on what the Bible teaches within the families or local churches? I think that kind of interaction is healthy. If biblical interpretation was so simple, we could feed the text into a computer and get the "correct interpretation." Now it may be true that ultimately there is only one correct way to interpret the Bible, but how do we find it? . . . I am, however, very willing to struggle to read the written Word through the eyes of the living Word.[1]

Interpreting the written Word, then, becomes our calling as we experience the Lordship of Jesus Christ in our lives. The written Word leads us deep into the faith journey of those who have gone before us. Through their lives and witness we continue to hear God speak the Word for our own day.

John R. Tyler, addressing a gathering of Cooperative Baptist Fellowship theological education partners in April 1977, spoke from a layperson's perspective on the needs of the church for theological education. His first point in the address was that "Fellowship laypeople need a sound theological foundation and the knowledge of how to apply it in a post-Christendom, post-modern world that is frightening to most of us."[2]

Tyler, in agreement with Weiss, understands that more than ever the church needs to hear the biblical Word. Tyler spoke of the ambiguity and lack of certainty that is replacing the solid rock upon which we have stood, and identifies the "fuzzy feeling that comes with the uncomfortable knowledge of a growing religious pluralism and what it means for our culture and our children and grandchildren; this creeping knowledge that the church seems to be losing her voice."[3] He calls for "staff members who will teach basic, foundational theology from the pulpit and in other creative church settings and then relate it effectively to contemporary life—not the life we wish Christians were experiencing, but to the life they are experiencing."[4]

The answer to the concerns raised by many in the church today is to return authentically to the biblical text and to pay attention to the Word in some new ways. The text itself holds the basis for claiming that it is the solid rock upon which we stand. That solid rock is a stable foundation that can allow for a diversity of reading strategies and theoretical models for interpretation of the Scriptures. We need to develop an increasing awareness of our own assumptions about the Bible and about our lives together as Christians, so that we can listen to others whose assumptions may well be different from our own.

MULTIPLE VOICES IN THE BIBLICAL TEXT

God cherishes each of the voices that comes from many places and many different perspectives. They are all part of the one human family. All human-kind are created in the image of God and are intended to fill the earth and have responsibility for it. Curtis DeYoung notes that the Bible addresses issues of diversity, but with emphasis on the oneness of humanity rather than on the differences within the human family.[5]

"In the beginning . . . " God's Word of creation stands as the first action in the Bible and includes the creation of one humanity. In spite of its own diversity, Israel affirmed the oneness of humanity in God's created order. Genesis 1:26-28 encourages all people to be in relationship to God, to under-stand themselves as created in God's image, and to receive the blessing given by God.

> So God created humankind in his image, in the image of God he created them; male and female he created them. God blessed them, and God said to them, "Be fruitful and multiply, and fill the earth and subdue it; and have dominion over the fish of the sea and over the birds of the air and over every living thing that moves upon the earth." (vv. 27-28)

The biblical Word is a paradigm for our understanding of the ways in which God works with the human family. Following the flood story, Genesis 9:1 repeats the blessing of Genesis 1:28. The human community is to be fruitful, multiply, and fill the earth having responsibility for God's creation. Yet, the very next story in the text is the tower of Babel (Gen 11:1ff). Nine short verses dramatically portray the way human sinfulness divides the human community and separates it from God's intentions for unity and wholeness. However, even the resulting dispersion of people into different language groups and separation from one another does not take away their essential createdness in the image of God.

The biblical story leads us to understand how humankind spread across the world and developed into different nations, languages, and cultures, and also affirms that God continues to call people into relationship. The ways of the world, the ways of attempted control on the part of human beings, leads finally to barrenness (Gen 11:30).[6] The scattering of peoples led to a decen-teredness in God, and peoples and cultures turned to other gods in hopes of regaining the center. Abraham and Sarah listened to God's call to turn away from the ways of the world. They began the journey to become the people who would show the world what it means to trust in God. The stories of our early ancestors in the faith in the book of Genesis (of Abraham and Sarah; of Isaac and Rebekah; of Jacob, Rachel, and Leah; and of Joseph and Asenath) testify to the ways they grew in the faith and shared that faith with others.

Thus, the paradigm story of the tower of Babel leads us to understand that our overwhelming self-importance separates us from God. The dispersed and scattered nations continued to grow and develop without the message of God's call. But Israel's location in the path between the ancient worlds of Mesopotamia and Egypt allowed this special nation to carry God's promise of blessing into interactions with other peoples. The trade routes that passed through the land of Israel, and the wars that waged back and forth across their territory, brought the Israelites the opportunity to know many different peoples, each of whom had developed their own history and religious assumptions. The Hebrew people learned who they were, as a nation and as a people of God, in contrast to the assumptions of these other peoples. Sometimes they were drawn to other religions, and sometimes they remained faithful to God's covenant, but always they worked and lived in the context of other voices.

During different times in its history, Israel experienced an intermingling of the peoples and an incorporation of those peoples into the Israelite community of faith. The Hebrews coming out of Egypt were a mixed group of followers of Moses, not just the immediate family of Jacob (see Exod 12:37-38). As they spent forty years wandering in the wilderness, they began to share stories of God's powerful acts in the community, and to be drawn together as a people who endured a common adventure. Their different backgrounds were woven into one story, the story of a faith journey in the wilderness. Yet, if we listen carefully, we can hear their voices, see the various threads that were woven together into one faith story. From the beginning of Israel's history, multiple voices spoke of God's faithfulness.

Even God's voice comes to the community in different ways. At Mount Sinai, this community came to know God through the lightning and earthquake, wind and fire (Exod 19–20). The people began the process of understanding what being in a covenant relationship with this God was all about. They experienced God in overwhelming natural phenomena. "On the morning of the third day there was thunder and lightning, as well as a thick cloud on the mountain, and a blast of a trumpet so loud that all the people who were in the camp trembled. Moses brought the people out of the camp to meet God. They took their stand at the foot of the mountain" (Exod 19:16). The people heard Moses speak and heard God answer him in thunder. Through the power of this mighty event, the community received the Decalogue, the Ten Commandments, and God's Word gave them the outline for living together carefully in community.

But there came a later time when the people became confused, for they thought the mighty power of the theophany was the only way God spoke. They assumed the storm god Ba'al also spoke in thunder and lightning. They heard others explain that the "Rider on the Clouds" was the one responsible for bringing the life-giving rain. And they worshiped Ba'al. So God sent the prophet Elijah to help the people understand that they couldn't worship both Yahweh and Ba'al. The people had to choose whom they would serve.

So, the prophet Elijah challenged the prophets of Ba'al for the people's allegiance. The contest at Mount Carmel (1 Kgs 18) resulted in the fire of God falling from heaven and consuming the offering Elijah had prepared, while the offering by the prophets of Ba'al remained cold and empty. Once again, through these impressive and terrifying events, the people affirmed their belief in Yahweh and affirmed their intention to choose God alone.

But the Lord was not done with Elijah. Threatened by the political power of the state to destroy, Elijah fled to Mount Sinai to receive again the directions of God for his life. But now a new theophany occurred. God was not in the overwhelming natural forces. God was not in the earthquake, nor in the wind, nor even in the fire, but in the "sound of silence"[7]—the still, small voice that directed Elijah to return to the world with new commissions to carry out. Elijah was sent back into the danger of political powers and principalities to lead the people out of their enslavement into the freedom promised by God's presence.

Is God either in the power of the mighty storm or in the sound of silence? The Bible affirms that God is in both experiences, for God does not come to us only in one way. Both experiences at the mountain are God's ways of speaking to us. We are awed to participate in the mighty events when we, like the people with Moses at Mount Sinai, sense God's presence in the power of natural forces. But those experiences are not all of God's mighty acts. We remember also to listen closely, for God speaks in the silent times, too. We sense God's presence in the quiet openness of prayer. Sent back into the world by God, we go, knowing God is with us as we journey into the newness of each day.

Through these examples we see the Bible as the record of many voices, speaking out in harmony and sometimes in discord. The authority of the Scriptures comes forth through the conversation among the multiple voices, not by suppressing or harmonizing them.[8] This kind of conversation occurs within the familiar story of Noah. In the telling of the story of Noah's ark, one community's story understood that Noah was to collect one pair of the unclean animals and seven pairs of the clean animals (Gen 7:1-5). Another community understood the number of the animals to be one pair each (Gen 6:19-20). The many storybooks about Noah on our own book shelves follow the story line of one pair of animals, and so we have chosen one biblical voice over the other. Nevertheless, the second voice remains in the text.

Even here in this small example are we given an either/or choice? The Bible says no, for both voices are appropriate versions of the Noah event. Both the 7-pairs/1-pair voices remained in the text as two understandings of the same event. When we read the text carefully, we find that the 7 pairs of animals were necessary because one community understood the importance of the sacrificial system as an appropriate form of worship of God. Noah offered a grateful sacrifice to the Lord (Gen 8:20) from the clean animals and birds, and the Lord responded with a renewal of the covenant. Thus, this voice is necessary as one interpretation of human response to God's saving acts.

Therefore, the Old Testament's multivocal and multivalent witness consists of the testimony that covers a time period of more than a millennium. This witness was formed in different languages and idioms and comes from different political and cultural contexts. As we recognize these varied witnesses to the actions of God with the community of faith, we see how the Bible reflects the dynamic relationship. This relationship between God and the faithful is intended to be resilient and responsive to changes in the human community while continuing to draw the community toward God.

MULTIPLE INTERPRETATIONS
IN THE CHRISTIAN COMMUNITY OF FAITH

When listening to multiple interpretations of the biblical text in our own day, we need to realize we have done our mission work well. Missionaries have brought forth the fruit of Christianity in the far corners of the world. We should not be surprised that people from backgrounds quite different from our own have interpretations of the Bible that also may be different from our own. We translate the Bible into many languages, go into all the world, and now, we are called upon to listen when others speak. Thus, on one hand, the biblical truth of "one human family, many cultural expressions" can be reclaimed and proclaimed in this age of diversity. God's love for all humanity does not change. On the other hand, the message of the ways people have responded to God's love keeps emerging in different voices.[8]

I have experienced the richness of others' perspectives. I began to get a glimpse of the power of listening to multiple interpretations through an experience of the worldwide church. The memory begins with an evening classroom filled with students whose Bibles are open to the stories of David, King of Israel and Judah. The classroom is a comfortable setting for me. Yet, in this room, the main language is Spanish—which is not a language I speak. Although the questions raised by the students are much the same as my students in Kansas City, some questions lead the class in different directions than I expect. The life experiences of these students who sit in front of me cause me to look with new eyes on a text I know very well. The questions and comments of the students at the Evangelical Seminary in San Juan, Puerto Rico, bring the written Word to life in new ways. These students are attending the seminary because they, too, have been called by God to preach the living word to people who hunger and thirst for the transformative possibilities of the love of Jesus Christ in their lives.

The next morning the translation consortium[9] comes together to discuss issues of bias in the translation of biblical texts. The diversity in the room has been deliberately gathered. We are a rainbow group who have been called from many places in the world—American and Asian and European and Hispanic, male and female, all shades of skin color, students and professors. The focus is on the Bible. We struggle to honor each other's experiences and to hear the direction from which each person approaches the Scriptures. Although I am uncomfortable with some of the perspectives in the room because they stretch my understanding of the Bible, I am aware that the Bible is able to stand in the face of our questions and our struggles with interpretation. We stretch each other as we listen carefully and speak with voices of people who are struggling with God's Word and taking its interpretation seriously for the church across the world.

Thus, in addition to hearing the multiple voices and concerns of the ancient communities reflected in the biblical record, we can also learn something about the Bible from contemporaries whose gender or social location has granted them different perspectives.[10] People have begun to raise up voices in the text that we have not heard before. We begin to see portions of the Bible that have been underutilized in sermons and studies, and so the content is unfamiliar. Perhaps it is time to listen to these new perspectives on ancient biblical voices. When we feel we are confronted with shifting sands within the church itself, whether from the voices of the postmodernists or those who speak from a post-Christianity perspective, or even from the secular ways of the world, we look again for that bedrock upon which we can stand. Yet, in this day, just returning to the Bible stories we know and love is not enough. We need to listen carefully to these voices and to place their struggles into a larger biblical understanding.

People around the world are hungry for the living Word, and they are searching for the "something more" in life. In our own society, people bring feelings and experiences with them to their search—feelings and experiences that are unacceptable in our churches, which may have caused them to be rejected by the church. Very often there has been an experience of hurt in the past by the very church people who are supposed to "love" them.

Our call, then, is to recover and to listen to some of the lesser-known voices in the Bible. These voices often are unknown or unfamiliar to us because the stories in which they speak or are silenced make us uncomfortable. These Bible passages do not fit our presuppositions of appropriate Bible verses. These voices occur in the difficult stories of rape, betrayal, and powerlessness. These voices often come from the women in the text, women whose stories are in the Old Testament (such as Jephthah's daughter, Hannah, the Levite's concubine, either Tamar, Rahab, Sarah, and Hagar, Miriam, and many others) and the stories of New Testament women as well (Mary Magdalene, Joanna, the woman with the flow of blood, Tabitha, Priscilla, Dorcas, Lydia, and many others). We are called to hear not only the women's stories—although they make up a good deal of what we have ignored in the biblical text—but also the voice of the slave, the voice of the outsider (the Ethiopian eunuch, the Queen of Sheba), or the prophetic voices of Amos and Micah.

Why should we listen to these voices? When we do listen and tell these stories, we bring a voice to the voiceless pain of life's devastating events. We place the whole of life into the context of the church and Scripture, and we learn new ways to respond to the shattering events of life. Thus, the church in our own day is obliged by the form of its Scriptures to listen for the voice of God in the dialogue of a community. The community recognizes the authority of the Bible and of God by continuing that dialogue.[11]

The community of faith is larger than our own congregation, or even our own denominations. The implications of the biblical story of the journey into faith are so monumental that one individual perspective, one denominational view, one cultural interpretation cannot come close to capturing its essence. As we open ourselves to listen to the Bible interpreted by people living in different local settings, with wide ranges of cultural experiences, we can gain a fuller understanding of the modern relevance of the ancient mysteries of God.[12]

So how do we do it? A model for creating a multicultural hearing for our understanding of the Scriptures means listening seriously to perspectives other than our own. The model includes placing a biblical text or theme in the center of our exploration, and then looking for ways to hear the text or theme from another's point of entry into the text. This method enables us to view concepts, issues, themes, and problems from several ethnic perspectives and points of view. This model facilitates the study of a passage from the perspectives of all involved in it and from several stances that interpret it.

Look again at the Exodus event not only from the perspective of the Hebrew slaves, but also from the perspectives of the Egyptians. We could listen to people who have experienced slavery to gain some understanding of the pressures our ancestors felt. We could tell the stories of the midwives or Moses' mother in addition to the story of Moses. Or we could look at the conquest of the land of Israel through the eyes of those who already lived in the land the Hebrews moved to possess. Interpretive perspectives from African-American, Native American, colonized Asian, and Hispanic women would add to the liveliness of the interpretation with which the text comes to life. The familiar verses all at once take on broader and richer meanings because of the addition of other voices to the dialogue.

But why should we listen? What does listening do for us? First, we deepen our understanding of themes in the biblical text to recover them from being ignored in our own culture. Native American theology can highlight our connections with the biblical theme of creation as seen through a correlation with Psalm 19. Psalm 19 speaks of creation and of the song of the created order in praise of God.

> The heavens are telling the glory of God, and the firmament proclaims his handiwork. Day to day pours forth speech, and night to night declares knowledge. There is no speech, nor are there words; their voice is not heard; yet their voice [chord/cord] goes out through all the earth, and their words to the end of the world. (vv. 1-4)

The Hebrew imagery in this psalm is the music of the spheres that are held together through the play on words between cord (a line to tie them together) and chord (the musical notes that form the harmonics). The psalmist declares that all of creation is interrelated and tied together.

Part of the interpretation of Psalm 19 is made clearer by Native American spiritual insights. Native American theology resonates with biblical concepts of harmony and order in creation, and the concepts are reflected in the basic liturgical posture of members of many North American tribes. DeYoung explains:

> Prayers are most often said with the community assembled into some form of circle. The circle is a key symbol for self-understanding in these tribes, representing as it does the whole of the universe and our part in it. All see themselves as co-equal participants in the circle, standing neither above nor below anything else in God's Creation. There is little sense of hierarchy in this cultural context, even of species, because the circle has no beginning or end. Hence all the "createds" (two-leggeds, four-leggeds, wingeds, and living, moving ones) participate together, each in its own way, to preserve the wholeness of the circle. The formation of the circle is itself prayer, a prayer for the harmony and balance of creation, and in some ceremonies no words need to be spoken.[13]

This Native American conceptualization of holy space highlights the interrelatedness and interconnections symbolized by the circle of prayer. Thus, we can develop a new understanding of the connectedness between the human community and God's creation through the new ways of thinking given by this cultural interpretation of the Bible.

Without the diverse perspectives of God's rainbow of humanity, we cannot grasp the true universalism of the biblical story.[14] God speaks to different communities, and they are able to grasp the word and hear its relevance to their own setting. We are able to spread the gospel into different lands because people are able to hear the truth of the message.

Sometimes we may not be able to understand certain aspects of the biblical story because we lack the necessary points of reference. We may miss the nuances that someone else can see clearly because his or her life experience is aligned more closely with that of the story being examined. We really do need diverse perspectives to gain wholistic understanding.

For example, the word *Calypso* is more than just a song in the Caribbean islands. Calypso is a word denoting a type of culture, one in which the element of folklore is dominant. Since in the process of interpretation of the

Scriptures, the culture of the interpreter influences the interpretation, what might be called "calypso exegesis" is influenced by folklore of the islands. In the words of George M. Mulrain,

> The calypso exegete, in his or her folk-cultured setting, is aware of the possibility of interaction or communication between the living and the dead. Calypso exegesis takes the spiritual realm and the demonic order very seriously.[15]

Dreams and visions constitute an important topic for calypso interpretation. Just as God is known to be revealed to people through dreams and visions in the biblical context, so it is with the calypso culture. Mulrain observes, "This fact may not be as striking among Christians within the denominations which have strong links with European churches, but certainly among indigenous religious groups, like the Spiritual Baptists of Trinidad and Tobago, this divine revelation through dreams is commonplace."[16] Thus, it is through the voice of calypso exegesis that we can begin to understand more fully the tensions in Saul's consultation of the Medium of Endor (1 Sam 25), Jacob's awe at his dream in Bethel (Gen 28), or Joseph's interpretations of dreams (Gen 40) and the influence that a belief in demons or psychic readers has in our lives.

In these ways, the various reading perspectives discern and identify sometimes overlooked aspects and accents within the Bible. These perspectives call attention to how these aspects have been strategic in the life and faith of the biblical community. As we can view them with openness, each perspective can inform us, raise our consciousness, advise us, and increase awareness of our mutual responsibilities as believers. The Bible is the property of the entire church, and each reading community within the church has insights to share with an interest to enlarge the church's vision of God and God's work among and through us in the world. The quest to understand and rightly utilize the Bible makes that sharing necessary.[17] We have heard the multiple voices of the past in the Bible. If it is to be a living document in the present, we must continue to hear the "new voices" of our day.

MULTIPLE VOICES ENABLING GOD'S SAVING ACTIVITY

God may well be doing something new in our own day. The world we live in has grown smaller as telephones, satellite access, and computers give us an ease of communication across the world that makes other countries as close as the next town used to be. Two of my friends in Topeka, Kansas, call their daughter to wish her a happy birthday while she is on a summer course in Paraguay. The Internet lets me access a library in Australia more easily than the one down the street from my home. Fax messages are read in church from our missionaries in the Philippines, and we learn that the church there has survived the previous day's torrential rains and flooding. We are connected today in ways that have the potential for increasing communication and possibly even understanding of others around the world.

Even in our own denominations and local churches, our community has changed in the last twenty-five years. American Baptist Churches USA have seen their commitment for inclusiveness manifest itself in the growth within that denomination through African-American, Hispanic, Native American, Haitian, Portuguese, and Asian American churches. If this trend continues, by the year 2000, there will be no single majority racial or ethnic group within the denomination.[18]

If we look to the population groups in our cities, we see a growing range of ethnic backgrounds. Latin Americans and Vietnamese give neighborhoods a different flavor along with new languages and experiences. Many churches are beginning to share their buildings with congregations of other ethnic backgrounds. Studies show that by 2056, for example, if present population levels and immigration patterns continue, Hispanic, black, and Asian people will together outnumber whites in the United States.[19]

Because we live in a world growing smaller, our neighbors may speak another language than English in their homes. We have different patterns of family life and assumptions about how to live together. Diverse life experiences create a multitude of beliefs about the ways in which the world works. Yet, the Bible is the constant for us in the Christian community. The Word of God remains as the connector, and in our diversity we are unified by a commitment to hold the Bible as authoritative within the community of faith.

Many interpreters of the Bible now come from cultures different from my own. How can we live in this world and understand the Bible without listening to the multiple voices of the variety of people with whom we come in contact every day? Perhaps we allow fear to limit us. We hold on to the known, for we are afraid of the unknown. How do we know that, if we listen to others' interpretations, we will not lose the center of our faith? Where is the rock on which we stand if others can hear voices in the Bible that we don't hear? Can I listen to them and still be true to my faith?

The good news in the Bible tells us that God is a God of the unknown as well as the known. Returning to the paradigm of the Exodus story, in

Exodus 16 we hear that following the powerful events of crossing the Sea and being brought out from slavery into freedom, the whole congregation of the Israelites complained against Moses and Aaron in the wilderness.

> The Israelites said to them, "If only we had died by the hand of the LORD in the land of Egypt, when we sat by the fleshpots and ate our fill of bread; for you have brought us out into this wilderness to kill this whole assembly with hunger." (Exod 16:3)

In the midst of their hunger, their fear of the future, and their longing for the old days of slavery, God provided. "Then the LORD said to Moses, 'I am going to rain bread from heaven for you, and each day the people shall go out and gather enough for that day'" (Exod 16:4). Whether it was manna or quail (vv. 13-16), God provided enough to satisfy that day's hunger. The people were learning to trust that God would be with them as they moved through the wilderness. Can we trust that God will provide enough for our needs in this day?

The good news in the Bible tells us that God is working in surprising places and with people even when we are not aware of God's activities. When the prophet Elijah arrived at Mount Sinai, God asked him what he was doing. Elijah went on and on in a speech about how he was the only one left of the prophets of Yahweh and that the powers of the world were seeking to take his life (1 Kgs 19:10, 14). But God did not allow Elijah to stay in retreat from the world. Not only did God's commission (vv. 15-18) send Elijah back into the midst of the political fray, but he was also commissioned to anoint his successor, and would find 7,000 people who had remained faithful to the Lord. God was working in the world, and Elijah was surprised to find many unexpected others who had remained quietly faithful to God's call in their activities. We, too, may be surprised at God's work in the world and by the many people who are remaining faithful to God's call.

The good news in the Bible tells us that God is relational and seeks to establish relationships with us. "For God so loved the world . . ." God's love encompasses each of us, and all of us. Are we called, then, to listen to others' experiences of God's love, even when they differ from our own experiences?

Where is God at work in our world? Where do we find the dynamic interplay of God's revelation through the written Word and the living Word? Is God inviting us to participate in a reformation of the communities of faith for this day?

CONCLUSION

The many voices we hear come from the past through our traditional interpretations of the biblical text to the present within the worldwide church.
These voices are bridged through the Scriptures themselves. Attempts to
defend traditional understandings tend to miss one essential character of
Scripture as a bridge between the past and present action of God. Yet, God
addresses new generations through words from the past. The expectation of
hearing a word for today, and thus a new word, is fundamental to the
church's understanding of the living nature of Scripture.

Scripture is both a product of tradition and a part of the church's ongoing tradition, and it cannot be interpreted as a document of faith apart from
that context of communal interpretation and use.

> Communal authority does not demand consensus, but it does demand
> engagement. The Bible exercises no authority for those who cease to listen
> or to struggle with it. While the degree of dissent tolerated by communities
> and individuals varies widely, unanimity of belief is not a demand of bibli-
> cal authority.[20]

Israel understood itself as a kingdom of priests and God's treasured possession. As a servant people, the call was for believers to be the leaders and
examples for the world. As we inherit this same call through the church, we
understand that the way is open for anyone who believes. No one is excluded
on the basis of race, gender, nationality, class, or culture. What matters is
faith in Jesus Christ. Therefore, we are able to walk the way, living into the
freedom granted by multiple interpretations of the biblical text.

NOTES

[1]Daniel E. Weiss, "Now, More Than Ever, We Need to Know the Word," Address
to the 1997 Biennial Meeting of the American Baptist Churches USA (June 1997) 1.

[2]John R. Tyler, "A Layperson's View of What Fellowship Baptists Need from Our
Theological Education Partners," Blowing Rock Retreat (28-29 April 1997) 2.

[3]Ibid., 3.

[4]Ibid., 4.

[5]DeYoung, Curtiss P., *Coming Together: The Bible's Message in an Age of Diversity*
(Valley Forge PA: Judson Press, 1995) 1.

[6]Walter Brueggemann, *Genesis, Interpretation: A Bible Commentary for Teaching
and Preaching* (Atlanta: John Knox Press, 1982): 116.

[7]Robert Coote, "Yahweh Recalls Elijah," in *Traditions in Transformation*, ed. Baruch Halpern and Jon Levenson (Winona Lake IN: Eisenbrauns, 1981) 118.

[8]DeYoung, 28.

[9]The Translation Consortium was sponsored by the Bible Translation Unit of the National Council of Churches to address issues of racial and ethnic bias in the translation of the New Revised Standard Version of the Bible.

[10]James Earl Massey, "Reading the Bible from Particular Social Locations: An Introduction," in *The New Interpreter's Bible*, Vol. I (Nashville: Abingdon Press, 1994): 151.

[11]Phyllis A. Bird, "The Authority of the Bible," in *The New Interpreter's Bible*, vol. 1 (Nashville: Abingdon Press, 1994): 63.

[12]DeYoung, 25.

[13]George E. Tinker, "Reading the Bible as Native Americans," in *The New Interpreter's Bible*, vol. 1 (Nashville: Abingdon Press, 1994): 176.

[14]DeYoung, 67.

[15]George M. Mulrain, "Is There a Calypso Exegesis?" *Voices from the Margin: Interpreting the Bible in the Third World*, ed. R. S. Sugirtharajah, new ed. (Maryknoll NY: Orbis Press, 1995) 43.

[16]Ibid., 45.

[17]Massey, 152.

[18]*We Are American Baptists: A Multimedia Magazine—1997* (CD-ROM).

[19]Cain Hope Felder, ed., *Stoney the Road We Trod: African-American Biblical Interpretation* (Minneapolis: Fortress Press, 1991) ix.

[20]Bird, 63.

Ministering in a Digital Age
Electronic Tools for Research and Church Administration

Donald E. Keeney

THE CHURCH HAS ENTERED THE TECHNOLOGY AGE. When my family arrived home after Christmas, I checked my e-mail and found there a message from a company I did not recognize. Friends at the International Baptist Theological Seminary in Prague had sent us an on-line Christmas card! I now receive voice mail via a new phone system at Central Seminary. Two of my colleagues work diligently with a long distance learning class using video, print, e-mail, voice mail, research over the Web, and various other sources. Our library is in the process of converting the catalog on-line to make it more accessible to faculty, staff, and students.

A local television station broadcasts worship services; a cable television network broadcasts services throughout the land. Videocassettes on many topics are available, for example, worship services featuring great preachers, episodes in the history of the church, and training sessions on how to carry out the ministries of the church. The use of fax machines and cellular phones is commonplace.

Some people in local congregations struggle to use technology well. There are opportunities for tension and misunderstanding. We need suggestions on how to use materials. Ideas can come from seminaries; other professionals, at county/area/state/regional/national levels or areas of service, one's own or other denominational meetings, laity, the community, public libraries, community colleges, and church-related colleges and universities.

The rapid technological development of recent years gives the Christian community tools to be faster, more efficient, and more productive. These tools affect us all as we participate in the work of the Kingdom of God. Yet these tools should cause us to pause and reflect on who we are, who God is, and how to be a faithful steward of God in the use of technology. The question is not whether we use technology, but how to use it to the glory of God.

Available Technological Resources

Increasingly, technology changes what we do in ministry and how we do it. Reporting technology becomes not a passive description, but an active invitation to minister better with faster tools and greater perspective. Computers make ministry in today's world a complicated task. They change how we study the Bible and how we find resources for ministry.

Ban, an international student from India, often logs onto the Internet and retrieves e-mail from his home. He is thankful for the convenience of keeping in touch with his family, but also finds that the resource tools on the Net are useful. He can look up materials from India, and search in a variety of dialects and even several languages. When information on the Net is too technical, he can locate definitions on-line as well. He has learned that not all information on the Net is current or informed. Some is well-intended, but lacking in perspective. Ban can find information about U.S. missionaries in India, and he can learn about ministries by Indian missionaries to the U.S. or Africa. He finds that people in the U.S. have been enthusiastic about missions, but have lacked the current information to be able to discuss or pray intelligently about India. Like many others, Ban has learned to take advantage of the technological resources available.

The Internet, for instance, can give us knowledge on how to minister cross-culturally, whether across town or across the world. Through e-mail and telecommunications technologies, we can be more aware of who is doing what ministry where. With the development of technology, missions volunteers can focus on service, not just conversion of the heathen. They can use their "secular" expertise to train Christians in other countries. Many retired persons have learned about foreign countries through advertisements on the Internet and, in turn, have volunteered for short-term missions projects.

On-line connections provide excellent resources using many technologies. The World Wide Web is the most popular on the Internet. Within the Web, several technologies also exist. The options are getting more complicated. Finding material on the Web can be a formidable task. The Web offers useful resources for ministry, but finding what you need can take training and effort.

Keep in mind, however, that the Internet is not a fixed resource. Information changes. Web addresses go out of existence. Some websites maintain dated information. Other sites relocate. Some add links to new sites and new information. New market segments are developing for

Christians who use different technological products and form different groups on the Internet, including computing, Internet services, and literature. Religious issues are gaining a hearing in the broader marketplace. From fundamentalists to evangelicals to mainliners to spiritualists who see the world as divine, religion is a growing part of the marketplace.

Currently, print materials (especially nonfiction books) are sold with CD-ROMs to indicate additional material, video clips, and updates about the subject (and now we have DVD). These combinations will become more complex as publishers of printed material use websites to update material.

The production of electronic texts is changing how we use printed materials. Printed versions allow us to read a narrative and understand its flow and ebb. Electronic resources can supplement paper ones. A printed text may have updated information on-line, or a CD-ROM may be packaged with a textbook to give an audiovideo interview with the author. Such works that integrate traditional print with electronic mediums set the pace for what is to come: new combinations of electronic tools that transform what we study, how we work, and how congregations work with professional staff.

Access to what the best are doing, edited and professionally edited, reviewed and polished, can create unrealistic expectations, but it can also give us a perspective for how we can do things differently, and maybe better. It can also create the expectation for entertainment.

Through the use of more audiovideo materials, churches have greater opportunities to record their histories and spiritual pilgrimages. Videotapes can present different ministries of a congregation, orient deacons to ministry, and present information about that congregation to newcomers in the area. Churches can use the Internet to share their reflections with others in the journey of faith and mission.

Similarly, wireless microphones are a part of available technology and have the potential to deemphasize the distinction between pulpit and pew and to invite a better sense of congregational participation in worship.

If we want to see how things will be in the future, we should look at the tools (or toys) for children. Children are using computers at very young ages. The new offerings increase rapidly. Many programs are available quite inexpensively. The programs have instructional dimensions; my son not only shoots asteroids, he learns basic mathematical skills in the process. The educational role of computers is so significant that a new term has been coined: "edutainment—for "entertaining" yet "educational" programs. These programs have several effects. They offer an alternative to television shows that often present little more than advertising in story form. They also shape the expectations of children as they mature. The programs of tomorrow will have to be lively as well as challenging and "entertaining." The same may be true for the church.

The challenge for congregations is to make available good videocassettes and computer programs as part of their ministries to children and their parents. Parents, other interested adults, and the wider community need to be involved in choosing materials. The church must realize that the next generation of Christians is growing up with these technological resources. Therefore, it has an educational and ministerial responsibility to make available challenging, exciting materials and, if possible, to assist in their production.

Most software is getting cheaper as it reaches wider markets. We must understand, however, that the need for more training is a human factor and a cost factor. These programs are tools, but they are tools that require ongoing training. They are not merely one-time expenses. The ongoing costs include updates to programs and to the operating system or telecommunications programs and the staff training times for any of these changes. The addition of every person affects the total network.

TECHNOLOGY AND THE SEMINARY

John uses the seminary library to locate materials for writing papers. He uses the Internet to look up books listed in his bibliography. He uses several key words to find a topic. He makes certain that the search engine uses all the terms, because often the default search string finds any one of the terms in a description. In researching the Internet for information on a church history topic, he had 200,000 hits, but only three were useful. He requested that those titles be held for him. He then looked in the periodical database for articles on his topic. The subject search terms were a bit different from the book catalog, but he found five magazine articles that looked useful. The seminary library had three of the magazines he needed, and he requested the other two through interlibrary loan.

In doing research, John also uses information from sites he considers useful. He has to use these carefully because some websites link to any one with a similar topic; others link to sites with a narrow social or political agenda. When John consulted the subject guide to church history at the seminary library, he clicked on a website and was transferred to a site at Vanderbilt University having a church history bibliography, video clips, and other sources. He visited other websites from there, returned to the guide at the library, and then found another site.

Sally, another seminary student, uses a computer to study passages of scripture. She consults several English versions and compares them. She traces themes in the passage and then the book, and looks at similar themes in the same genre. Then she looks up the Greek or Hebrew word or phrase in the original language. She checks the meaning in the New Testament and compares the word or phrase with other synonyms using a Lexicon based on semantic domains.

Sally then compares her thoughts with information she finds in commentaries on a CD-ROM. Next, she consults other commentaries in print and considers some of their broader themes. She rereads the scripture text to determine its impact on the original hearers, and then develops a message to deliver the same impact on her audience. Again she consults commentaries and compares her results to the ideas of other writers.

Finally, Sally constructs a message and compares it with other results on the Internet. She finds examples of sermons, audio clips of an oral interpretation of the text, and video clips of a drama. She posts her work at the school's website and then answers e-mail about how she thought to use this idea, resulting in conversations with people she has not met.

The experiences of John and Sally are not uncommon. They have used tools commonly used by scholars in days past, but they have used them in different ways. They have used both print and on-line resources. They have looked at many different resources, some with considerable caution. They have developed their own perspectives and conclusions, and their work becomes the basis for other ideas.

The experiences of John and Sally also illustrate some of the advantages and problems with electronic texts. For word searching, computer programs help tremendously. For ease of use and comparison between several translations, as well as in Greek and Hebrew, they are unbeatable. But such ease of use can be deceptive. Not all programs use the same search techniques. Further, these programs do not seem to be used alone. They are part of a combination of print and electronic texts. This is especially true of broader areas of research. It is almost as if they have two overlapping markets. Electronic encyclopedias seem to be replacing printed ones. *World Book Encyclopedia*, for example, is now available on CD-ROM at a fraction of the cost of the paper edition. Sales have dropped dramatically for general reference encyclopedias, but they have soared for electronic editions. As a reference work, it is easier to use an electronic edition that delivers specific articles quickly than it is to find an article in a paper edition. But for texts in general, electronic works do not seem to be at the expense of sales of traditional printed texts. Each year 35,000 new books are published, and the trend continues unabated.

Managing information in all its various forms is complicated and will become moreso for three reasons. (1) There will be much more information; (2) it will come in more varieties; and (3) it will be more mixed. More information means many choices: videos on what it means to be a Christian, books on how to think intelligently about issues, and websites with updated material on a number of concerns. But more information will also mean there will be much more "junk" to wade through. Some will be well-intentioned, but lacking in thought. There is therefore a need for a way to sort the good from the bad and the useful from the distracting.

Consider the recommendations of magazines, websites, and colleagues. *Christian Computing* regularly reviews Bible study software. Also consult *Computing Today* (from *Christianity Today*) and *Church Bytes*, soon to be retitled *Scroll* (from Deerhaven Press). *The Atlantic Monthly* blends print, electronic media, and coverage of religion and society. The market for Christian material in a secular marketplace is such that programs for the Christian market are now a regular part of general trade publications. *PC Magazine* regularly reviews Bible programs. *Publishers Weekly* reviews religious fiction. In addition to consulting magazines and websites for recommendations on good materials, you or someone in your congregation may want to meet on a regular basis with others who share similar but not the same interests. County-wide denominational or ministerial meetings provide good opportunities for discussion about useful programs. E-mail correspondence with friends and colleagues can also be useful.

Some sources think only electronic texts are good; others think print is best. To many young people, electronic texts are more authoritative, even if an item in print is more recent. In fact, different uses will develop according to needs. Printed books are not going away, although the numbers of electronic texts are increasing. The two sometimes create new services. IBM now has a service by which out-of-print books can be scanned and then printed in a small quantity. Studying the Bible will continue to require skills in reading print as well as skills in database text management. The use of computers will change how we read, however. The result will be a blend with electronic for some uses and print for others. Another blend will allow us to read some materials more closely while allowing us to be more selective of which parts of other works we read.

Technology and the Local Church

Eleanor is the librarian at her church. It seems that there are two or three libraries in one room: one for adults; one for children; and one for videotapes, CD-ROMS (with movies or interactive games), and audiotapes. There are also different types of equipment to use with these media.

The church library works with the public library to make as complete a collection as possible. The public library has some useful general interest items, but cannot keep church training materials. The church library has more materials for Sunday School and includes some perspectives that call people to make decisions according to sound Christian principles. The public library provides useful material for making some of these decisions, but the church library can be more openly confessional. The computer in the church library has an on-line connection to the local library. This connection is not on the Internet, which is available in the church offices.

The church library also has lists of materials contained in other church libraries, including new titles. Most of the cooperating libraries are of the same denomination, but some are of other denominations. A few are independent churches. It is amazing to Eleanor that so many issues seem to cross denominational lines. She is particularly impressed by the CD-ROMS at the Methodist church library. One CD-ROM contains a book of worship, scripture readings, and a hymnal.

David, a lay member of the church, is interested in finding more materials on Baptists. He looks in the church library and gets some help. He looks up sites on the Internet and finds the home pages of the American Baptist Church and the Cooperative Baptist Fellowship. From there he skims documents and then downloads them into files on his computer for later reading. He uses links to the Baptist Peace Fellowship and the Baptist Joint Committee on Public Affairs. He visits a local Baptist college and uses its materials.

David decides he would also like to have information on ministries in local churches. He looks at his own church's webpage, checks links to other local sites, and finds a mass of material on the web that tends to be promotional literature. He skims these and finally uses some terms for the specific ministry he is looking for. He combines these terms with his previous search strategies and finds some useful information. He discovers that other local congregations are doing similar work, but he has some distinctive ideas he thinks would be useful. He sends e-mail to the staff and deacons of his church, gets responses, and makes a presentation at a Wednesday evening meeting at his church.

Sarah works in the office of a church with a large staff. She responds to e-mail the ministers forward to her and in turn coordinates their task load. E-mail has improved communication with church members, but it has complicated the office tasks. The newsletter is sent by regular mail and e-mail. The worship bulletin is available on-line to members before the printed copies are in the mail.

The office personnel and ministers at this church use a complex software package that requires regular updates and training. The staff uses the congregation's database for many things. It tracks contributions quite well, making it easier to detect trends in designated giving. Ministers also use the database to analyze trends in the local community as a basis for future ministry.

In addition to using e-mail and office software, Sarah coordinates the use of other technology. Audiovisual media are often used in one of the worship services. The visual images contribute powerful imagery to some of the worship experiences.

As technology develops, congregations will work to use it well as a group. Individual expertise is good, but technological companies that flourish do so because they listen to and respond to people's concerns. Technology in the church must assist in no less.

Congregations can use different media to bring about an orchestrated result. An upcoming mission trip could be supplemented by a video from the last one and reinforced by announcements in the newsletter and through e-mail.

Increasingly congregations will rely on computer and communications specialists. In particular, they will need technical specialists who are sensitive to the nature of churches and the way they work. Church leaders will count on "laity" to make things work, thus involving more laity in the ministry of the church.

How congregations make use of technology will change. Phone systems now make it easier to communicate within the congregation. Voice mail makes it easier for staff members to communicate. E-mail makes written notes easier to work with. As office systems develop, the clergy will be able to communicate better with church folk and vice-versa. This communication will become a basis for church members to participate more fully in the work of the congregation. They will be able to minister alongside the clergy.

It is important to remember, however, that automated procedures can mean greater stress on people. There can be a problem when the automation of a machine does not match the existing procedures of the church office.

Sometimes who gets to use which printer can become a spiritual question: is it the person with the longest tenure or the most forceful personality? Attention must be given to the human and social dimensions of what computers do. Remember, the goal of the church is service in community to the Living Lord, not individual efficiency at the expense of others.

Obviously, technology adds several dimensions to office dynamics. Unfortunately, technology has the potential to have a dehumanizing effect on people. It can put constraints or ease of use on the easiest or quickest way to do things when instead we need reflection and perspective. As ministers, we need to help others use their gifts in applying technology to the needs of the church. We also need to use our gifts to teach others how to use technology appropriately, individually, in staff or committee or building projects, and as a congregation. People need to be involved in the process of choosing which software to use. The software chosen should contribute to better human-ness, not less. Members of the congregation also need to be trained in how to use the software. These ethical issues stem from our theology of priesthood of believers. We are priests to each other. Office systems must incorporate that priesthood.

CONCLUSION

There is a need for more thought about what technology does to people. Some of the people who speculate on these trends are labeled "Futurists." There is even a Society of Religious Futurists. On the congregational level, we all know individuals who are so involved with computers that their personal skills are lacking. In an office, technological choices have a profound impact on personal dynamics. It is at least a requirement that those who deal with technology be included in decisions about the technology they use. What may seem useful to a highly skilled individual may not be useful to a group of people for whom technology must be useful. Training in an initial setup and in the ongoing use (and updates) of programs is essential. Ongoing evaluation of technology and how people use it must be part of standard operating procedures.

Likewise, the church must keep in mind that not all technology is useful for everyone. We must ask ourselves: How does the technology contribute to worship or congregational planning? Perhaps we need a theology of computer usage. Although deciding which computer piece is often a matter of economics, using technology relates to issues in human relations, administration, and theology because it is a part of the question "How do we minister together?" This question requires reflection by clerical and support staff, and should become part of the mission statement of the church and its staff.

Decisions about technology affect the entire group. Appropriateness of filenames can change. With the addition of a new person, network access may need to be modified, and access to a common printer, telephone line, or on-line service may change. For these reasons, as many people as possible need to be involved in the process of change.

As stewards and servants to our people in culture, we have a responsibility to learn to use technology well. We must learn it with purpose—from the perspective of servanthood, to enable everyone to use their own gifts well in service to God in Christ.

Robin,
I am
thankful to
be your colleague
and sister.

SPIRITUAL FORMATION
THE JOURNEY TOWARD WHOLENESS

Molly T. Marshall

Xρις,
Molly T. Marshall

"SPIRITUALITY" IS A HOT TOPIC. A review of those books that have enjoyed a sustained tour on the *New York Times* bestseller list over the past few years is liberally sprinkled with books on spirituality. It is not just "religious folk" who use the term, either. Management techniques in corporate structures, leadership theory, even the coach of the Chicago Bulls resorts to some notion of spirituality to seek to transform players who present a significant challenge. "Spirituality" has become a booming industry and is avidly marketed alongside other "self-help" enterprises. Burgeoning literature, "chant CD's," "vision quests," corporate "mission statements"—all point toward a deep spiritual hunger permeating American culture. Obviously, all that claims the word "spiritual" cannot pass for Christian spirituality.

Until about a decade ago, most persons in the free church tradition, especially Baptists, knew very little about spiritual formation. (Some perhaps thought it was early morning exercise at camp to ensure "firm believers" or walking in a straight line to required chapel at a Christian college). "Formation" was thought to be an exclusively Catholic term, a regimented preparation for those with a vocation for the priesthood. It entailed adopting a "rule," a careful methodical approach to spiritual disciplines that shaped the whole life of the seminarian. Attending to one's spiritual formation was deemed in this context as important as learning biblical exegesis, homiletical skills, theological and liturgical history, and pastoral care.

Baptists, schooled in the voluntary principle, have rightly resisted any coercive dimension of Christian faith; however, their stress on the priesthood of all believers has both exacerbated individualism and contributed to a wariness about spiritual direction or guidance from another Christian. Thus, the idea of formation as an intentional receptiveness to a set of Christian practices, guided by a more mature Christian, has not been sufficiently a part of Baptist catechetical structures.

Further, the Protestant Reformation's insistence on *faith alone* has, unfortunately, fostered a deep suspicion about the efficacy of any human effort in matters of salvation. "Only believe" became the watchword of those shaped by a tradition that accented the justifying action of God to the neglect of "growing in grace," the transforming movement of sanctification. In addition, the Reformed tradition has treated the biblical idea of perseverance as a logical corollary of God's unilateral election; therefore, "working out one's salvation with fear and trembling" has not been viewed as the essential expression of personal redemption.

Alongside this theological legacy is our acquisitive culture's preoccupation with achievement, programmed outcomes, and easily won certitude. Give us the formula, the opinion of the expert, or the right software, and we are certain we can solve the problem. Thus, the acute spiritual longing of contemporary persons is vulnerable to purveyors of spiritual methods that promise quick solutions to the unfathomable emptiness that characterizes the spiritual lives of many, even among those who claim Christian identity. The idea of a patient, receptive, collaborative process in which one's true spiritual identity is forged over time seems strangely out of sync with today's instant communication, instant credit, and instant gratification.

Attentiveness to the interior life, long the staple of monastic life, is gaining ground among Baptists. Retreat houses are full; spiritual directors are in demand; academies of spiritual formation are flourishing; even Baptist seminaries are seeking to design curricula that will prompt new emphasis upon what students are becoming—not just what they are learning. "Mastering (or mistressing) the body of divinity"—what used to be the goal of theological education—is now sharing the stage with a more reflective look at the connection of the whole of human life as spiritual with the One whose image we bear. The cynical refrain "Keep it in the cloister; it won't work in the demands of real life" is being replaced by a new appreciation for ancient forms of spiritual disciplines and community, through which contemporary Christians are experiencing a new sense of transcendence and divine companionship in their daily living.

This chapter examines spiritual formation, especially in light of Baptist understandings of salvation and the church. Four affirmations frame this treatment: (1) formation is God's work and ours; (2) formation is a lifelong process; (3) formation actualizes our calling as truly the image of God and truly ourselves; and (4) formation happens best in community.

FORMATION AS A DIVINE AND HUMAN WORK

Spiritual formation is not all God's work, nor is it entirely up to us. Seeking to retain this delicate balance has perhaps sparked more heated theological debate than any other area of Christian doctrine. Influenced by the Lutheran condemnation of "works righteousness," the Reformed accent on God's electing grace, and the Wesleyan stress on methodical and stringent forms of discipleship, Baptists have teetered between an activism that seeks to "build up (if not bring in) the Kingdom" and a kind of quietist approach that simply believes God's providence will work its way ineluctably, with or without our help.

It is helpful to recall that the Protestant Reformation was not only a reform of theology; it was also a reform of spirituality. Significant aspects of monastic life such as spiritual direction, regular confession, rites of penitence, and communal accountability were swept aside by the flood of Protestant concern about the abuses of these practices. The Catholic tendency toward legalism and moralism, with the concomitant fear about never doing quite enough, was met by the Protestant "corrective" that assured God's work of grace required nothing of the Christian but faith—which could never be considered a "work." Skeptical of synergism, the idea that God and humans work together, Protestants have conducted a protracted discussion on the relationship of justification to sanctification, especially the beginning and continuation of salvation.

It is not easy to articulate the way in which divine sovereignty and human responsibility interface. Particularly difficult is discerning the mode of God's action in human life. Does God's activity displace ours? Do our efforts at faithful following of the way of Christ mean that we are not dependent upon grace, that we are attempting to *earn* our right-standing with God? How do the prevenient (antecedent, anticipatory) actions of God call forth responsive human collaboration?

Before attempting to answer these questions, it is important to note that spiritual formation speaks of a two-way movement: God's quest of us and our quest for God. The biblical material is unequivocal: God has been seeking us long before we feel our lack and begin to search. Scripture and life experience also suggest that without seeking we are unlikely to find God, and that the human quest for God can only succeed because God desires to know and be known by us. We do not "find" God by dint of sheer determination. How, then, do we relate the action of God to the action of the human in spiritual formation?

One way of characterizing the relationship is this: It is all of God, and our human responsibility is simply to be thankful for God's mighty works. A key prooftext for this position is Ephesians 2:8-9: "For by grace you have been saved through faith; and this is not your own doing, it is the gift of God—not the result of works, so that no one may boast." This approach encourages passivity on the part of the believer; he or she simply must try to stay out of the way of God's working. Often persons characterize as miraculous God's unilateral and intervening work; God can do whatever God chooses no matter how the human supplicant prays, keeps covenant, or holds trust. The main problem with this understanding is that human participation is seen as a hindrance to God's work; God's sovereignty leaves no room for human cooperation. Thus, it diminishes the human to mere spectator in the cosmic process. Further, crediting God with the only action that matters leads to a determinism that not only lauds God for all good that occurs, but also blames God for evil. A satisfactory theodicy cannot be forged by following this pathway, nor can there be a clear concept of spiritual formation.

Another way of understanding how the actions of God and humans interface, popular in contemporary liberal theology, is what I call "radical immanentalism." This concept simply means that human actions are God's mode of acting, and God's actions are dependent upon human actualization of them. Rather than asking God to provide for the homeless, concerned persons ought to set about making this provision themselves. While this incarnational principle of Word becoming flesh as God's means of action in the world can prompt robust discipleship, is this the only way God can be at work in this world? The problem with this approach is that God's capacity to accomplish the divine will can be utterly thwarted by uncooperative humans. To limit God to this extent collapses the distinction between the divine and the human. A favorite prooftext for this perspective is Paul's exhortation: "Work out your own salvation with fear and trembling" (Phil 2:12), and persons who believe that God "has no hands but our hands" attempt such work with alacrity. The harder they work, the more spiritually formed they become, or so they imagine.

A third, more promising, way is to speak of the concursive action of God and humanity. God's action undergirds and makes possible human action. They can work simultaneously with neither displacing the other. God's grace is still prior to human participation, proving "love for us in that while we still were sinners" (Rom 5:8), and the Christian knows better than to confide in his or her own strength to "become obedient from the heart"

(Rom 6:17). Yet there is a mysterious mingling of the life of God with the life of the one whose "life is hidden with Christ in God" (Col 3:3). The Apostle gathers up this idea with his declaration: "I have been crucified with Christ; and it is no longer I who live, but it is Christ who lives in me. And the life I now live in the flesh I live by faith in the Son of God, who loved me and gave himself for me" (Gal 2:19b-20).

When considering the processive movement of spiritual formation in the life of the Christian, it is best to use this third model. It acknowledges the ongoing transforming work of the Spirit and pays attention to the mode of God's presence in the life of the believer. Biblical metaphors for the Spirit as Comforter, Teacher, and Encourager suggest that the personal presence of the Abiding God respects the personhood of a saint in the making. The functions of the Spirit as Interpreting Voice, Reliable Guide, and Empowering Friend are characterized by a certain humility and ineffability, so that the movement of divine presence cannot easily be distinguished from human choice and deed. God's humility establishes our dignity.

As a divine and human work, spiritual formation depends upon God doing for us what we cannot do for ourselves and our doing what only we can do. We cannot save ourselves from the wages of our sin; we cannot become who we long to be by ourselves; we cannot generate from within the human race a Savior for the world. Christian faith rightly proclaims: God bears the cost of our sin on the cross; God wraps a "robe of righteousness around our pig-befouled bodies" (Luther); God sends/comes as Jesus the Christ to open a "new and living way" (Heb 10:20). It is the divine prerogative to redeem rather than condemn. In mercy, God purposes to save and never ceases working to that end, as Jesus testified (John 5:17). This is God's work.

What responsibility for spiritual formation is dependent upon our work? Actually, quite a bit. Even though we would confess that the Spirit of God is at work in the heart of every person who has confessed Christ as Lord and been plunged into his life through our baptism, our receptivity and practice of certain disciplines can open up the channels through which the Spirit is free to perform Her transforming midwifery.

Scripture enjoins us to seek, study, serve, and be still. We shall treat each of these briefly in turn. Lyrically put to music by Mendelssohn, the prophet wrote: "If you seek me with all your heart, I will let you find me, says the Lord" (Jer 29:13b-14a). Seeking God grows out of being oriented toward God, something God has crafted into the very fiber of our beings as human; indeed, we are restless until at home, at peace, with God. Echoing Jeremiah,

Jesus exhorts: "But strive first for the kingdom of God and his righteousness, and all these things will be given to you as well" (Matt 6:33). We are to be intent on discerning the weightier matters. We were created with the desire to know, to search, to understand. Too often, we limit our search to the phenomenal—that which we can perceive and measure with our senses. Yet there is something within us that quests to understand the noumenal—that which calls forth the seen and gives it depth and interprets its meaning.

The luminous gift of mind, with which we are beckoned to love God, demands study. One of the first instructions about study a Baptist child learns is "Do your best to present yourself to God as one approved by him, a worker who has no need to be ashamed, rightly explaining the word of truth" (2 Tim 2:15). To be formed spiritually requires being instructed in the Scriptures. We must let the written word of God take up lodging in our hearts, letting it form our minds and transform our actions. We listen for the voice of Christ to order our steps. We must probe the Bible's stories to learn rich insights into the character of human beings. In addition, we must not neglect the rich heritage of Christian literature, classics of Christian devotion that are suffused with enduring perceptions about Christian discipleship.

Spiritual formation in the Christian tradition means becoming ever more like Jesus through following him and imitating him. He described his mission in terms of a "downward mobility": "For the Son of Man came not to be served but to serve" (Mark 10:45). Our service, like his, is cruciform in nature. When we think too highly of ourselves and look only to our own interests (Phil 2:3-4), we cannot follow the One who willingly took "the form of a slave" (v. 7). We must with vigilance put to death those self-protective impulses that make us resistant to the needs of others, that cordon off their claim on our attention and time.

Another discipline, which tempers the activism of these others, is receptive stillness in the presence of God. The contemplative stream of spirituality has not been mainstream in Baptist perceptions, perhaps due to the Protestant dismissal of much of their pre-Reformation heritage. The scholastic penchant of the later Reformers, and their appetite for rationalistic doctrinal formulations, had little use for the more inward experience of encounter with the Holy. Scripture urges another form of knowing than that which can be gleaned from study: "Be still, and know that I am God" (Ps 46:10). The heart of the contemplative tradition is its insistence on paying attention to the presence and movement of God in all things. Patient attentiveness makes possible a deepened awareness of the ways God nudges and blesses. Indeed, most humans miss the wonder of the media through which God makes divine presence palpably known because they have not cultivated the capacity for silence in a noisy world.

Spiritual formation is not externally imposed, nor is it individually accomplished. It is a cooperative venture that requires an ever-deepening fidelity to the truth about ourselves as beloved of God. The next three sections, albeit shorter, will necessarily depend upon the theological construction of divine-human synergy.

Formation as a Lifelong Process

The spiritual "Lord, I Want to Be a Christian" intones a yearning to become what we profess. For some, this is rather disturbing. If we have accepted Christ, why should believers be troubled about being "like Jesus" or "more loving" in their hearts? Isn't that a given? We may be alarmed to hear that we are to *strive* to become fully Christian, since we are taught that we are saved not by our own goodness, but by God's grace alone. Of course it is all of grace; yet there are practices and understanding that will allow God's grace to become more effective in our lifelong following of Jesus.

Baptists have tended to truncate the salvation experience by accenting its beginning to the neglect of "growing in grace." Knowing the precise time one "got saved" thus has been the functional doctrine of assurance for this brand of evangelical faith. The inaugurative event of conversion was the consuming concern. Repentance was seen as past tense (hence, post-baptismal sin placed a question over the authenticity of the salvation "experience," an age-old problem in the church); confession had been completed in the acknowledgment that "Jesus is Lord"; and particular practices that demonstrate one's new identity as a Christian really could not add anything to what had already transpired, lest there be suspicion that the work of grace was insufficient. Baptists, in particular, have been adept at getting children baptized, but we have been less successful in nurturing mature faith. Instruction was aimed at getting one to make the initial faith commitment, not toward a discipleship that could weather the developmental challenges and crises that are a part of the life stages of adolescence and adulthood.

James Fowler offers a helpful overview of the stages of faith.[1] After conducting an extensive study of the belief structure of persons of faith, he and his team of researchers described some developmental patterns that have chronological as well as intentional implications. In other words, some of the shifts he describes come naturally as one matures as a human; others come about only by intentional reflection and openness to change and growth.

The desert monastics of the fourth and fifth centuries had a peculiar wisdom we have forgotten. They believed that all of life's circumstances were a means of spiritual instruction and possible transformation. They also believed that true Christian living could only be forged over time. Listen to these snippets of insight:

> Abbot Ammonas said that he had spent fourteen years in Scete praying to God day and night to be delivered from anger.

> An Elder said: "The reason why we do not get anywhere is that we do not know our limits, and we are not patient in carrying on the work we have begun. But without any labor at all we want to gain possession of virtue."

> Abbot Palladius said: "The soul that wishes to live according to the will of Christ should either learn faithfully what it does not yet know, or teach openly what it does know. But if when it can, it desires to do neither of these things, it is afflicted with madness. For the first step away from God is a distaste for learning, and lack of appetite for those things for which the soul hungers when it seeks God."[2]

Each of these sayings reminds us of the patient labor required to habituate Christian virtues into one's daily concourse. While God's work of grace in our lives continues, we can be obedient to its impulses by our attentive discipleship.

Some lessons in Christian living can be learned only in the midst of life's most bracing challenges. Her confidence in the provision of God can only be refined when she walks through the fires of losing her livelihood. His trust in God's unfailing mercy is restored when the estranged son returns to be reconciled in the father's declining years. Whether an interruptive crisis or the particular task of developmental stages, all of life's experiences can be a means through which we learn more about the mercy and faithfulness of our God.

The Scriptures exhort us to pursue this pilgrimage of faith with perseverance, trusting that what is "not visible" will come because God can be trusted in our living and in our dying. Hebrews 11 sets before us a panorama of women and men seeking a homeland, for whom "greeting the promise from afar" was sufficient to sustain their journey. Surrounded by these witnesses, we too run the race that is set before us, looking to Jesus (Heb 12:2) throughout our lives.

From beginning to end, our lives are oriented toward God who invites us to make our home in eternal communion with the divine, triune community. It will take our whole lives to let go of our presumptions about achievement and to learn that we are formed spiritually by what we are willing to receive.

FORMATION AS CALLING TOWARD TRUE IDENTITY

Christian theology teaches us that all humans are called to bear God's image in the world. Because of human refusal to live in abiding communion with our Maker, our true identity has been diminished. We have turned our faces away from the One whose glory we were meant to reflect. Salvation is a processive healing of the chasm created by sin, a beckoning to know as we are also known, a seeing face to face. Turning toward the divine visage mediated by grace allows us to become truly God's and truly ourselves.

A key to understanding our true identity as Christians lies in plumbing the depths of our baptism. While I will say more about the corporate dimensions of this formative confession of faith in the next section, at this point we need to focus on baptism as that which tells the deepest truth about our lives.

Baptists have tended to view baptism as *imitation*. Because Jesus was baptized, we are also to be baptized. This is not an adequate view from the perspective of the New Testament, which gives a much more profound interpretation to this reorienting act. Our baptism is *incorporation* into Christ's baptism; by the power of the Spirit, what has been disclosed in his dying and rising includes us. It is the truth of our lives, too. Romans 6:3-4 declares:

> Do you not know that all of us who have been baptized into Christ Jesus were baptized into his death? Therefore we have been buried with him by baptism into death, so that, just as Christ was raised from the dead . . . we too might walk in newness of life.

Hence, the Christian cannot understand himself or herself apart from being utterly identified with Christ.

Other texts extend this idea of our identity being formed through our union with Christ. The practice of putting on a new garment following baptism, a wonderful symbolism of new life, illumines the Galatian metaphor of "clothed yourselves with Christ" (3:27). Further, Romans 8:29 describes the goal of Christian personhood as being "conformed to the image of [God's] Son." Perhaps most graphic is Paul's teaching in 2 Corinthians 3:17-18 that we are being transfigured into the glorious likeness of the One we are beholding "with unveiled faces." God created us to become like Jesus, one who lived for God and for others out of the fullness of his distinctive life.

The paradox of grace (to use Baillie's beloved depiction) is that while we are becoming truly God's through Christ, we are also becoming most truly ourselves. The work of the Spirit in the life of the Christian is to set her or him free to express all that wells up through the distinctive personhood given/forged over time. One's true giftedness is liberated from stultifying self-interest, and its expression becomes an oblate, an offering of the whole self to God. We were meant for this kind of openness to God and others, "created in Christ Jesus for good works, which God prepared beforehand to be our way of life" (Eph 2:10).

Spiritual formation, thus, is a divine-human art form; it is a composition, a sculpture, a tapestry, a dance. It is about turning away from the worship of gods created by human hands and turning toward the One who makes all things new, that by "turning and turning we come round right."

FORMATION AS THE WORK OF CHRISTIAN COMMUNITY

In the construction of Christian creeds, how to speak about the church was always a lively issue. Although the doctrine of the church only became a source of real controversy during the Reformation, before that time the question of how properly to relate the church to belief was of concern. Christians confessed their belief *in* Jesus Christ as a chief article of faith; in wisdom they came to understand that they did not believe *in* the church in quite the same way. No, they argued, it was more important to believe the church's teaching than to have faith in the institution itself. The church thus served as the matrix in which faith occurred; it provided oversight to the practices that shaped Christians: sacraments, confession, singing, Bible study, and service.

"No one can be a Christian alone," wrote John Wesley, clearly understanding the need for community in learning to be obedient to grace. Our Baptist forebears also understood the community as essential to Christian identity. English Separatist John Smyth came to the correct insight about our organic relationship to other Christians: Since no one gives birth to oneself, no one ought to baptize oneself. Being joined to Christ is inseparable from being joined to members of his body. Contemporary Baptists link baptism to church membership, and there is a certain wisdom in that as long as we do not forget that Christ's body is not coterminous with the Baptist form of being Christian.

The church provides our introduction to the stories of the Bible. Earthy in its realism, biblical characterizations offer pathways to follow and pathways to avoid. From it we learn to confess our sin and believe in God's forgiveness. From it we learn the contours of Jesus' ministry and how our lives are to be patterned after his. The regular study of the Bible in Sunday School, its proclamation in worship, and the encouragement to personal, devotional reading all express the church's unique relationship with Holy Scripture. The Bible affords the interpretive framework for our understanding of creation and redemption, life on earth and life in heaven. Its narration of promise and fulfillment ensures our confidence in the God whose character it renders in both surprising and reassuring ways.

The church in worship also forms us spiritually as we learn to pray, sing, and celebrate the sacraments as the gathered community. Prayer as sharing life with God, Roberta Bondi's description,[3] is learned primarily through hearing prayers in worship. Private prayer is watered by the springs of public prayer. We learn the form and content of prayer by being led by others; corporate worship thus serves as a school of prayer in spiritual formation. Singing our faith is a distinctive Christian practice. "Faith is born and lives in song," writes Don Saliers.[4] Perhaps the hymnal is the closest thing to a book of worship that Baptists possess. Because hymnody has such powerful capacity to shape theology, it is imperative that we select hymns for congregational use wisely and that we be attentive to new hymns, many of which are much more concerned for inclusivity and social justice in this world. The metaphors used for God have powerful capacity to order human relations, and many contemporary hymn writers are especially gifted in stretching images and functions of the divine.[5]

Rarely have Baptists given the sacraments (or covenant signs, or ordinances, if you prefer) their due. Relegated to a minor role in worship, we have neglected their powerful efficacy in spiritual formation. In word and rich symbolism, they order a congregation according to the paschal rhythms of the new life in Christ. Layered with meaning, baptism and eucharist move us toward an embodiment of our shared life as the people of God. It is crucial that we celebrate these together and often, for "we must continually strive to learn in the company of our sisters and brothers what it means to be a people that are reconciled and reconciling, forgiven and forgiving."[6]

The community is necessary to spiritual formation, for there we find reliable guides in faith and practice. While the calling of Christians is to imitate Christ, we can be helped immensely by those whose lives have been patiently disciplined through years in his fellowship. In the memorable words of Albert Schweitzer:

> And to those who obey Him, whether they be wise or simple, He will reveal Himself in the toils, the conflicts, the sufferings which they shall pass through in His fellowship, and, as an ineffable mystery, they shall learn in their own experience Who He is.[7]

Congregations are usually a repository of saints. Ordinary people who have allowed the Spirit to plow the soil of their hearts live out of a fullness of grace that is winsome to behold. Wisdom—often hard-won—humility, and a certain expansiveness of heart characterize these who have long practiced their faith. They mark out the path before us, and we do well to heed their example.

One ordinary saint from my home church in Oklahoma was a significant part of my own spiritual formation as a child; and his witness continues to influence me as an adult. He worked as a county extension agent, an agriculturalist and animal husbandry specialist who assisted farmers in the county with stock and crops. A generous man, he had some land out of the city where he regularly invited children from the church and his neighborhood to go and ride horses, work in the barn with him, ride in his old pickup truck, and most important, simply spend time with him on the land he loved. Saddling up horses for "city kids," arranging wiener roasts at the ranch, teaching us in Sunday evening discipleship training, we experienced his interest and care for each of us. On Sunday mornings you would find Mr. Denton in his regular place, the second pew from the front on the south side of the sanctuary. Not surprising, his pew was always full of kids. Most welcome were those who did not have a father in the home or who were marginalized in some area of their lives. Now, forty years later, this kindly man still finds time to drive a church bus, gather up children needing his attention, and show them the face of Christ through his simple, yet profound actions.

We are all called to be saints and, according to John Wesley, it will not come to pass unless we *intend* to become saints.[8] The community of faith is the context where our lives are bound together by the Spirit of God, who uses every aspect of our common life as a means to form us spiritually.

*****

In conclusion, we have considered the four aspects of spiritual formation in this brief essay. It is a divine and human work, it will take our whole life, it brings us to our true identity, and it requires the community of faith. Each suggests a way that Baptists (and all Christians) can be more intentional in their responsiveness to God's work of grace in our lives.

NOTES

[1]See James Fowler, *Stages of Faith: The Psychology of Human Development and the Quest for Meaning* (San Francisco: Harper & Row, 1981).

[2]These brief sayings can be found in Thomas Merton's collection, *The Wisdom of the Desert* (The Abbey of Gethsemani: A New Directions Book, 1960).

[3]I have been helped immensely by Roberta Bondi's work *To Pray and To Love: Conversations on Prayer with the Early Church* (Minneapolis: Fortress Press, 1991).

[4]Professor of Theology and Liturgy and director of the Master of Sacred Music program at Candler School of Theology, Emory University, Saliers contributed the chapter "Singing Our Lives" to the significant new collection *Practicing Our Faith: A Way of Life for a Searching People*, ed. Dorothy C. Bass (San Francisco: Jossey-Bass Publishers, 1997) 183.

[5]I am thinking especially of the work of Thomas Troeger, Ruth Duck, Brian Wren, and Jane Parker Huber.

[6]"Re-Envisioning Baptist Identity: A Manifesto for Baptist Communities in North America," *Baptists Today* (26 June 1997) 8-10.

[7]*The Quest of the Historical Jesus* (New York: Macmillan, 1906) 403.

[8]See John Wesley's generative work, *A Plain Account of Christian Perfection* (London: Epworth Press, 1955).

Theology and Ethics
Commending Christian Faith in a Postmodern World

David L. Wheeler

My formal training is in systematic theology, or, as we have called it in our curriculum at Central Baptist Seminary, "constructive" theology. In this theological discipline, we build up a connected system of doctrinal assertions meant to express, in their consistency, coherence and comprehensive scope, a Christian view of the world and the human situation in it. The challenge of constructive theology is not limited to the professional theologian. Every thinking Christian is a "theologian in residence" in his or her own life situation, charged with making sense out of life in the light of Christian faith convictions, and commending the faith to our neighbors. "Always be ready to make your defense to anyone who demands from you an accounting for the hope that is in you" (1 Pet 3:15).

In recent years I have also begun to teach and write in the field of ethics. Ethics is the systematic exploration of human behavior with respect to the goals and values that inform it. I see a natural connection between the two disciplines of theology and ethics, at least as they are pursued in the context of Christian faith. One's most deeply held convictions about the nature of God, the world, and humanity will—to the extent that one is self-conscious and purposive about one's actions—guide one's behavior and form one's character. And one's behavior will, over time, critically and constructively impact one's core beliefs. Thus, for a Christian believer, theology and ethics are involved in a mutually conditioning feedback loop.

Because they are thus related, theology and ethics are impacted in today's intellectual and cultural climate by the same fundamental challenge. Traditional Christian thought is thoroughly *foundationalist*. The foundationalist seeks some enduring point of reference, some preeminent reality, on which to base convictions about the broader world and its value. Baptist theologian Stanley Grenz puts it this way: "[W]e believe that there is a unifying centre to reality and that this centre has appeared in Jesus of Nazareth."[1] Such foundationalism is not the exclusive property of classical Christianity.

Indeed, the history of Western thought can be understood as the "search for a firm foundation." Rationalists ancient and modern have thought that belief and action can be founded on the deliverances of pure reason, abstracted from the accidents of culture, convention, and our physical natures.[2] Modern empiricists have restricted meaning to the deliverances of the senses and have attempted to conform behavior to the conditions of the physical world displayed by sense data.[3] Alike in their differences, traditional rationalists and traditional empiricists are foundationalists—as are classical Christians, who make God's self-revelation in nature, in the self, and, ultimately, in the Word made flesh, Jesus Christ—the foundation of all meaning and value.

A broad and pervasive contemporary intellectual movement threatens foundationalist schemes of all kinds at their very roots. Sometimes called "postmodernism," sometimes called "deconstruction" after the terminology of the French philosopher Jacques Derrida, this movement has many faces. In ethical thought, some postmodernists question the existence of any enduring, transcultural "good." Applied to the physical sciences, deconstructive thought interprets "natural laws" as conventional and utilitarian. And, most challenging for classical Christianity, in which God is an eternal, unchanging reality who is knowable to humanity through a revelatory *Word*, the philosophy of deconstruction denies fixed, enduring meanings to words.

R. Albert Mohler expresses the *scriptural* foundationalism typical of evangelical thought: "The Christian tradition understands truth as established by God and revealed through the self-revelation of God in Scripture. Truth is eternal, fixed, and universal."[4] But for the deconstructionist, a word once uttered, or even a word enshrined in a text, is no longer the "property" of the utterer, but is endlessly malleable, subject to reappropriation and transformation or even inversion of meaning for as long as it continues to be re-uttered, re-heard, or re-printed.[5] In the hypertext culture of the computer age, even "classical" texts enshrined in bound volumes, even "Holy Scriptures," lose their untouchability and their coronas of officially attested meaning.

This challenge to permanency of meaning and certainty of value is not simply a characteristic of truth-weary academics. Popular history today trashes national icons. Popular opinion seeks out and believes the worst of public figures in every field, including the leadership of the church. The contours of morally accepted lifestyles and relationships are custom-tailored to every interest group and constituency, or—alternatively—"traditional values" are trumpeted and flaunted simultaneously by their very defenders.

Protestant Christianity was born with the battle cry of "*Sola Scriptura!*" American Evangelicals, in particular, have characterized themselves as "People of the Book," followers of "the Word." But the "Battle for the Bible" has been moved to a potentially treacherous new playing field in our generation. Since the Enlightenment, says reformed theologian John W. Cooper,

> The tactic of some apologists has been to adopt modernism's rationalistic standard of truth in order to argue against modernism that reason actually supports rather than undermines Christian truth claims.[6]

Practically speaking, this has often taken the form of fashioning a network of propositional truth claims out of the fixed canon of Scripture and comparing these claims with those of competing systems for adequacy to the facts of experience and illuminating power for living. But what form can such an *apologia* take when the question about the Word is not about its trustworthiness with respect to other words but whether *any* word can be an enduring basis for community building and principled living. Or, to put the challenge more broadly, before Christians can proclaim Christ and his word as the foundation for living, we must ascertain if there can *be* any foundation.

The Reigning Paradigm: Describing Modernism

Before we describe in more detail "postmodernism" and the challenges it poses to Christian faith, we need to characterize the "modernism" to which it is—in all of its many forms—reacting. Recognizing our own most natural convictions and standards of intellectual operation as being particular and historically conditioned—in our case, "modern"—is not an easy exercise. It is somewhat akin to a fish being consciously aware it is swimming in water. Nevertheless, we need to name and become aware of the key factors at work in our native thought world.

Critical Consciousness

Ted Peters describes the modern mind as one that has emerged into *critical consciousness*.[7] That is, it no longer accepts unquestioningly the received wisdom of its own or any other culture—whether that wisdom is expressed in ethnic or national sagas and ideologies, structures of power and authority, or the culture's sacred texts. The emergence of this critical consciousness was a function of one of the two great paradigm shifts in the history of Western philosophy, one taking place at the dawn of modernity and proving crucial to its development, the other taking place in our century and serving as a midwife to *post*modernism. The first of these great paradigm shifts produced modern critical consciousness precisely by elevating *human reason* to ascendency over all traditions, canons, and authority figures.

The Primacy of Reason

This first great revolution received classical expression in the work of Rene Descartes (1596–1650), and is often called by philosophers "the turn to epistemology." Epistemology is the branch of philosophy that examines the conditions of our knowing. Prior to Descartes, the great philosophers were preeminently concerned with the question of *being* ("ontology") and the issues of moral virtue and behavior that arise naturally when we attempt to correlate behavior with what truly *is*. Whether one was an "idealist"—believing that ultimate reality is mental or spiritual, and the material world is derivative and secondary—or a "materialist," like so many modern thinkers, philosophers assumed that humanity *can* obtain direct and accurate knowledge of the real world. Such a faith is not just a philosopher's conceit; ordinary men and women on the street yet today operate with a naive, common-sense realism: "What I see is what is really there, and what is really there is what I see."

Descartes, in his famous *Meditations,* set out to systematically doubt this common-sense realism.[8] Rather than take for granted the deliverances of the senses or the existence of God or any of the received wisdom of the race, he found himself able to doubt it all, *except for* the fact that *he*, the thinker/doubter, by the very fact of his thinking and doubting, *was*. The autonomy and self-authenticating nature of human reason thus became the cornerstone of global modernity. I, by virtue of my own self-conscious, analytical operations, am my own authority—not tradition nor cultural mores nor sacred scripture.[9]

The Scientific Revolution

In the wake of Descartes, philosophy was no longer primarily about the nature of *being* but about the conditions of *knowing,* and thus about how the human intellect might master and utilize its environment for its own well-being. So one might understand *the scientific revolution* of Francis Bacon, Isaac Newton, and others as a natural accompaniment of the

Cartesian revolution. Descartes had distinguished between self-conscious, analytical *thinking* substance (human souls) and lifeless, inert *material* substance. In Cartesian thought, the nonhuman world loses the aura of awe and spiritual power with which premodern cultures typically invest it, and becomes mere raw material, to be manipulated and exploited pragmatically for human comfort and security. Modern science and technology are based upon the examination and manipulation of material reality by autonomous reason. And the search is not for some ultimate "truth," but for what *works*, whether to explain or to exploit.

PHENOMENALISM

Science relies on empirical data, the fruit of observation. But one who has absorbed the lessons of Descartes' *Meditations* can no longer simply accept sense data at face value. Modernism sees sense data not as exact reflections of the world as it is in itself, but as functions of the interaction between the knower and the known. What we experience are *"phenomena"* (appearances), which are constructed at the interface of a presumed real world "out there" with our human structures and categories of knowing. According to this philosophical "phenomenalism," which received its classical expression in the work of Immanuel Kant (1724–1804), we can know that such categories as "time" and "space" and "cause" are part of our human way of knowing, but we cannot know if they are characteristic of the world in itself.

This meant that a great gulf of uncertainty separated human knowers from the material world they manipulated and exploited through science.[10] Rather than a quest for truth, modern philosophy, including what Enlightenment thinkers called "natural philosophy" (our "natural science"), became "pragmatic" in nature, that is, a quest for what *works*. The autonomous self, the "I" on its throne, might not enjoy the certainties of premodern societies, but it was the arbiter of its own values and loyalties. And where philosophy led, business, statescraft, and religious life followed, and global modernity spawned a culture of appearances and game plans in place of certainties and principles.

MODERNITY AND CHRISTIAN APOLOGETICS

It is not surprising that our Christian experience and our understanding of Christian faith have been profoundly shaped by modernity. The rootage of Christian faith in scripture and ancient ecumenical tradition, and two millennia of vastly varied expressions of the faith in vastly varied cultures, have kept it from being resolved without remainder into modernity, but the modern influence has been profound.

For one thing, modernity's canonizing of the autonomous *individual* led Christian preachers and theologians to read the biblical narratives as *the many stories* of individuals seeking salvation, rather than *the one story* of God's universal redemptive plan. Furthermore, the rationalism and empiricism of the modern critical consciousness cast biblical miracles and the traditional picture of a supernatural God into grave doubt. Early in the modern era such thinkers as Thomas Hobbes and Baruch Spinoza insisted that the Bible be analyzed like any other human document, and be subject to the same canons of literary and historical criticism wielded by an autonomous reason.

One might usefully interpret Christian theology in Western Protestantism and Roman Catholicism as taking one of two great options in response to modernity. *Liberalism*, as pioneered by the thought of Friederich Schleiermacher (1768–1834), tended to replace the authority of scripture and creed with the authority of personal experience. Since critical consciousness cast the supernatural into doubt, defense of the faith retreated from the forum of public reason and history to the forum of personal testimony and in-group experience. All of the contemporary "theologies of experience"—feminist, liberationist, black, mujerista, and so on—are genetically related and descended from Schleiermacher's rooting of apologetics in "Christian consciousness."[11] But because they all move in the sphere of influence of modernity, evangelical theologies as well as liberal theologies and New Age doctrines appeal heavily to personal experience for their credibility.

On the other hand, *Evangelicals* as well as traditional Roman Catholics have responded to modernity in a dramatically different fashion. In response to modern rationalism, they have insisted that Christian faith rests on objective, public data, in the manner of the physical sciences, in making its faith assertions. Christian claims about the being, the character, and the creative and redemptive activities of God are understood to refer not merely to subjective experience, but rather to the larger world of history, both human and natural. In evangelical thought, scripture is mined as a data base to substantiate these claims, much as a physical scientist would test hypotheses and substantiate claims about the natural world from physical data.[12] When modern critical consciousness attacks scriptural authority, this type of theology responds that the comprehensive worldview that it develops from biblical data is more adequate to commonly acknowledged facts of public experience than alternative views.

The irony of these tactics is that both liberal and evangelical apologetics are using elements of the modernist paradigm to defend a faith tradition whose original supernaturalism and wholism are radically at odds with modernism. Liberalism exalts the individual and private experience, while for biblical faith the individual's very identity is a function of God's calling, and individual well-being is a consequence of the universal *shalom* of God's Kingdom. Evangelicalism, while also casting divine redemption in individualistic terms, attempts a public *apologia* by abstracting supposedly universal laws from a body of evidence, as do the modern natural sciences. Yet the biblical God is like the wind that "blows where it chooses" (John 3:8), and His Word resists being squeezed into the straitjackets of our doctrinal systems.

As creatures of modern culture, we find that our apologetics are modern to the core. And thus we are caught in a dual dilemma. We are wedded to apologetic principles and strategies that may be, on the one hand, compromised in their integrity because of their commitment to an incompatible paradigm, and on the other hand, compromised in their effectiveness because of their commitment to a paradigm that is passing.

The New Paradigm: Describing Postmodernism

There have been two great paradigm shifts in the history of Western philosophy. The first brought into focus the role of the *knower* in our encounters with the world and was a midwife to modern critical consciousness. The second great shift began at the turn of the 20th century with the work of logicians such as C. S. Peirce, Gottlieb Frege, and Bertrand Russell.[13] These thinkers began to analyze the role played by *language* in the human encounter with the world.

Like Descartes and Kant, they were acutely aware of the role our knowing structures and procedures play in shaping our assumed knowledge of the world. But modernism could argue that "knowing structures" such as our senses are innate and uniform for all human beings. In contrast, these "poststructuralist" thinkers understood language to be radically contextual. Susan Brooks Thistlethwaite describes this position:

> In addition to the view that human subjectivity is constructed by language, poststructuralists believed that language itself is not fixed but "built," as

words acquire meanings in specific historical locations. These locations are always the site of competing meanings and, hence, of struggle.[14]

To cite a notorious contemporary instance of this struggle: the "truth" about the football hero, television personality, and accused murderer O. J. Simpson has been a shifting will-o'-the-wisp continuously produced, deconstructed, and reconstructed by whatever linguistic community was interpreting him—prosecuting or defense attorneys, the mainstream media, the tabloid press, racially-divided public opinion. . . . It would seem that Simpson himself had a very illusive and impermanent sense of himself and his personal responsibility since so much of his "self" was out of his control and in the linguistic public domain.

If we human beings are "constructed," as selves, in language communities that are ever struggling and evolving, then it would seem that the *modern* understanding of the self would be subject to strenuous challenge. And to the extent that our rational appropriation and defense of our Christian faith has been shaped by modernism, our faith, too, will be challenged.

Thus we will now return to the several characteristics of modernism described earlier and examine how the emerging *post*modern paradigm is challenging these principles.

CRITICAL CONSCIOUSNESS AND THE AUTONOMOUS SELF

In modernist thinking as modeled by Descartes and Kant, the autonomous, rational *self* becomes the judge of the validity of information about the world, values, and moral prescriptions. Descartes, in his exercise of systematic doubt about his own sensory data and his interpretation of it, finally found certainty about his *knowledge* in the indubitable nature of his own mental processes. Kant made the rational self, abstracted from any particular community or even any hint of emotion, the arbiter of *moral principles* in his famous statement of a universally applicable moral principle, the "categorical imperative."[15]

In the landscape of postmodernism, the modern critical consciousness has turned upon itself, resulting in "the dismantling of the centered and unified subject."[16] Our century has seen a nightmare of wars; conflict among ideologies, generations, and genders; and a cultural climate that makes us doubt our values, our rationality, even our very identities. In such a climate, the self ceases to appear as a relatively stable entity, defined by its own rationality, and takes on the appearance of a tenuous "trace." Mark C. Taylor, one of the most influential of American postmodern thinkers, visits the dictionary to define this key postmodern concept of the "trace." And yet it defies singular definition.

> Trace: a course, path, road, or way; a way of life . . . To trace: to take one's course, make one's way; to proceed, pass, go, travel; to pass along or over; to traverse; to follow the footprints of; to copy . . .[17]

So what can we say about the self as "trace"? To be a postmodern self is to be a process or to be on a journey, and to be subject to, responsive to, even in a sense to emerge out of the ever-changing network of conversations, activities, and relationships that encompass us. To be a postmodern self is also to be radically open to the challenge of "the other"—the one who is other than us by reason of speech, gender, values, culture, ideology. The postmodern self is not self-contained, complete and certain about things, and can no longer take for granted even the most cherished and seemingly self-evident principles of its own social and linguistic environment. Even in the articulation of cherished convictions, the traces of the other "will manifest themselves as fissures, gaps, paradoxes, and incongruities on the surfaces of their expressions."[18] For example, who today can recite Thomas Jefferson's words in the Declaration of Independence about "life, liberty, and the pursuit of happiness" without seeing the haunting eyes of Jefferson's black slaves?

This postmodern understanding of the self as "trace" leads to an understanding of human history as, in Taylor's words again, an "erring." While biblical pilgrims go on a journey where the uncertainty of the destination is counterbalanced by the certainty of God's providential leading,[19] the postmodern pilgrim is a wanderer who "moves to and fro, hither and thither, with neither fixed course nor certain end."[20]

PHENOMENALISM UNLEASHED

As the critical consciousness of modernity turns on itself in postmodernity to deconstruct the centered self, so the phenomenalism of modernity turns upon itself in postmodernity to evacuate historical assertions and scientific theories of any fixed and certain reference. They are seen as merely useful *tools* for organizing data and making practical predictions. And since our theories may or may not "work," and even if they do work may have unforeseen negative consequences (e.g., negative environmental fallout from technological advances), the modern faith in history as making progress toward some future utopia begins to go by the boards. It is no wonder, then, that postmodernism is haunted in many of its expressions by a "sense of *irrevocable* loss and *incurable* fault" and an "overwhelming awareness of death."[21] On the other hand, there does emerge from time to time in this rhetoric of the "trace" and "erring" a sense of playfulness, a wistful hopefulness. There are simply no guarantees as to outcome.

POSTMODERNITY AND CHRISTIAN APOLOGETICS

How Postmodernity Challenges Liberalism

Liberal Protestantism responded to modern skepticism about traditional, supernaturalistic Christianity by grounding its apologetics in natural, presumably universal characteristics of human selves. Schleiermacher postulated that underlying the mixture of partial dependency and partial freedom of agency that characterizes all human beings in our networks of relationships, there is a universal "feeling of absolute dependence" that finds its fulfillment only in relationship to God.[22] In our century Paul Tillich similarly linked basic Christian doctrines to widespread human longings and feelings of disquiet. For instance, the Christian experience of "new being" (="salvation") correlates to well-nigh universal human feelings of "estrangement" from our best and most essential selves.[23] These modern thinkers connect with an ancient and honored tradition of apologetics exemplified by Saint Augustine, who identified universal longings in the mirror of his own individuality and uttered a famous confession of human need for God: "My heart is restless until it finds its rest in Thee."[24]

I have already raised questions about the validity of liberal apologetics with respect to core biblical themes. But liberal strategy will also find itself radically questioned by postmodern thought. On the one hand, postmodernism's themes of "irrevocable loss and incurable fault" would seem to resonate with the themes of "estrangement" and "alienation" in the work of thinkers such as Tillich. But for postmodernism, human alienation is typically reinforced and radicalized by the corollary of the death of God, whom we are understood—after Feuerbach and Nietzsche—to have created for ourselves "in our own image." There is no longer a privileged perspective, or an ultimate and final judge, in the world of postmodernism. In contrast, Taylor speaks of "the empty space that frames our circumstance" and "the silence of Jesus."[25] In the century of Auschwitz and Hiroshima, it seems that the postmodern heart finds *no* rest. The freedom to go erring is freedom *from* God.

Furthermore, quite apart from the God question, liberalism's characteristic appeal to the human self as center of experience and arbiter of its value runs smack into postmodernism's deconstruction of the self. As David Griffin puts it: "The idea of an autonomous, self-determining, centered self is regarded as an illusion to be 'deconstructed.' "[26] For postmodernism, the self, construed as an ephemeral stream of experience, can neither preserve and transmit fixed truths nor be the beneficiary of a permanent "salvation."

How Postmodernism Challenges Evangelicals

The contextual theologies of experience that developed from the liberal tradition acknowledged the varieties of human experience; humanity is legion! Postmodern thought pushes even further to dissolve "humanity" into multiple traces of experience. But however pluriform humanity is conceived to be, our experiences are both structured by and encoded in *language*. *Evangelical* apologetics, as we know, centers in the *Word* of God. But this Word and its authority are not self-referential. The Word is derived from and refers to the real, personal God who is its author. Even if the postmodern thinker grants this reference of the Word, the same objections to the permanence of character and autonomy of experience that postmodernism brings to the concept of the human person will apply equally to a divine person. Is our *Yahweh* the tyrant who declares a genocidal war upon the inhabitants of Canaan (cf. Josh 6) or the loving God and Father of our Lord Jesus Christ who is not willing that any should perish (Matt 18:14)? Who, finally, is to say?

Furthermore, whatever our concepts of God's character and activity, we reference them in a *text*. And postmodernism understands texts in radically different ways than traditional Christianity. Taylor speaks of our words as "an unending play of signification."[27] Words have no unchanging, universally accessible and agreed-upon reference. Is "justice" the same for the slaveholder and his slave? Is an "economic expansion" the same thing for the investment class and for hourly wage earners? Is the "promised land" the same for the Israelites and the Canaanites? "There seems to be no exit from this labyrinth of interpretation. Everything is always already inscribed within an interpretive network."[28] And these interpretive networks are functions of our own group identity, our own vested interests, so that—as Corduan said—"truth is seen as being defined by those who have power in society."[29]

Words, whether spoken or written, always partake of this malleability of reference. But inscribed in a text, words continue to mean in ways perhaps completely beyond the ken of the author. For instance, is the story of David and Jonathan's surpassing love (1 Sam 18) an illustration of courtly mores in the early Israelite monarchy, an early example of "male bonding," or a landmark literary trace of committed gay eros? Or can it be all of these things and more? Who is to say? The postmodern interpreter would deny both a single, univocal, permanent interpretation to this text, and the existence of any authority competent to declare such an interpretation.

In sum, from the perspective of the postmodern critique of the centered self, the absolute Self (God) and the text with clear reference and determinate meaning, a typical evangelical apologetic, consisting of uniquely true propositions abstracted from a privileged text, seems not only intellectually indefensible but also—what's worse—a procedure inevitably infected by the self-interests of the powerful.

And yet, could it be that the sword of deconstructive postmodernism, which seems so destructive of traditional Christian apologetics, both liberal and evangelical, might be a *two-edged* sword, both wounding and freeing as it cuts? John Caputo, an important American interpreter of the European tradition of deconstruction, says:

> The very meaning and mission of deconstruction is to show that things—
> texts, institutions, traditions, societies, beliefs and practises of whatever
> size and sort you need—do not have definable meanings and determinate
> missions.[30]

So far, this seems to be a perfect statement of deconstruction's skeptical, corrosive effect on biblically-based faith. But Caputo continues: "that they are always more than any mission would impose, that they exceed the boundaries they currently occupy."[31]

I am reminded again of Jesus' words in John's Gospel: "The *pneuma* [wind/spirit] blows where it chooses, and you hear the sound of it, but you do not know where it comes from or where it goes" (3:8). And again, "I still have many things to say to you, but you cannot bear them now. When the Spirit of truth comes, he will guide you into all the truth" (16:12-13a). We would squeeze the Word that we call "Word of God" into our determinate formulas and systems, to protect our traditions and institutions and afford ourselves security. But Jesus characterizes God's self-communication as moving, uncontrollable, and still in process. God, through the Spirit, will have a word for every context and situation. Is it not precisely at this point that Christian apologetic theology might begin to glean important insights, both substantive and strategic, from the tenets of postmodernism?

RESPONDING TO POSTMODERNISM BY LISTENING TO JESUS

Sometimes the person, movement, or state of affairs that we perceive as "the enemy" can be our best teacher. Christian faith can never embrace the intellectual and moral relativism that seems to characterize deconstructive postmodernism. In contrast to its strenuous critique of all foundations, we confess that "no one can lay any foundation other than the one that has been laid; that foundation is Jesus Christ" (1 Cor 3:11). But postmodernism's insistence that all communication—symbols, words, texts, communicating persons themselves—has an overplus of meaning that cannot be pinned down or captured in abstract formulas, can help us to redirect defense of our "foundation," and better understand its nature.

The foundation is not Holy Scripture *per se*, conceived of as a collection of propositions with fixed interpretations, which we can completely understand and permanently apply to any conceivable situation. Nor is it any particular system or tradition of theology. Rather, the foundation is the *living Word*, Christ Jesus himself, continuously present to us, in us and among us through the Holy Spirit. "Now the Lord is the Spirit, and where the Spirit of the Lord is, there is freedom" (2 Cor 3:17).

Diogenes Allen reminds us that in deconstructive thought "there is no universal system."[32] But we Christians don't, or at least shouldn't, worship a "universal system," or even the dream of one. Instead, we worship a universal Christ, whose creative power and redemptive love have been and continue to be present in every world culture, whether recognized and acknowledged or not (cf. Col 1:15-20).[33] Across the centuries, loyalty to Christ has produced Augustinian and Thomist, Calvinist and Wesleyan systems, each attempting in their own ways to mirror the richness of Christ and make his presence real and effective in their own settings. Allen continues: "We live in a pluralist, not a provincial age. This is not to be lamented. It frees us from dogmatism and we have a choice between various options. Options mean freedom."[34]

Thus the "constructive" or "systematic" theology that we do as pastors, teachers, and "theologians in residence," seeking to be clear, consistent, and truthful in our own settings, will be more open, less defensive, and more celebrative of new life and new possibilities in Christ. Indigenous churches in Latin America, Africa, Korea, and around the globe are asking questions and rereading scripture in new and different ways that go beyond the vocabulary and categories of our European-American Protestant tradition.[35] We should celebrate these new expressions and learn from them. Still, I insist that, postmodernism notwithstanding, there is and always will be a foundation for authentic Christian faith. But the foundation is a person, not a set of doctrines.

The New Testament lifts up Jesus Christ as both the normative person, into whose full humanity we are drawn by faith (Phil 3:12-20), *and* the human embodiment, in our common human history, of the eternal God (John 1:14; Col 1:19). His compassionate actions, his healing and reconciling power, and his announcement of God's new age of universal *shalom*, constitute the interpretive key uniting the diverse themes of scripture, and authoritatively define for us the character and will of God. The person Christ Jesus is a living interpretive norm for our willing, speaking, and doing—whatever our cultural setting.

Of course, if our faith is grounded in a *person*, we must acknowledge that postmodernism has strenuously criticized the modern notion of the rational, autonomous person, and has insisted that the self is fluid, and linguistically and culturally "constructed." But in this light it is interesting to reflect how the biblical notion of the self is itself critical of the modern paradigm. Scripture does not define the self by virtue of certain constant and independently possessed attributes such as rationality. Rather, as we were reminded a generation ago by neo-orthodox thinkers such as Karl Barth and Emil Brunner,[36] the human person is constituted by *the creative call of God*.

> For it was you who formed my inward parts; you knit me together in my mother's womb. . . . In your book were written all the days that were formed for me, when none of them as yet existed. (Ps 139:13, 16b)

In addition, the "image of God" in humanity consists not in the possession of certain attributes unique to human beings. Contemporary biologists tell us that the ravens calculate and the apes mourn their dead. But rather, our being in God's image consists precisely *in our ability to respond to God* and to live out our divine callings before God:

> Before I formed you in the womb I knew you, and before you were born I consecrated you; I appointed you a prophet to the nations. (Jer 1:5)

As we ponder the nature of persons, we remember our question about the nature of the Divine Self: "Who, finally, is to say?" Ted Peters reminds us that all of our would-be answers are in the nature of wagers, but he characterizes Christian symbols as "reality detectors"[37] that can flush out the constant and the true in a world of personal "traces" and historical "errings." Peters says:

> The God of Israel is mysterious on many counts, but one salient feature of the revelation in Jesus Christ is that this is a God of faithfulness.... The divine voice has spoken to us through the prophets and through the Son with the message that a new and transformed world is coming, where swords will be beaten into plowshares, lions will lie down with lambs, and there will be no more tears in our eyes. Now this claim is either true or it is not. The Christian faith is constituted by trust that it is true.[38]

The philosopher Derrida speaks of faith as the basic trust posited in every act of communication. "You address the other and ask, 'believe me'." Such a stance of faith is "absolutely universal" and absolutely necessary if one is to persist in living.[39] *Everyone* in our evermore complex global culture will continue to invest basic trust in somebody or something, or else humanity would simply cease striving and cease to be. In Christ, God is addressing the world and saying, "believe me." Christian faith historically has shown the flexibility and the power to speak authentically to cultures on every continent, and to transform them toward *shalom*. Times change; languages evolve; human cultures flourish, intermingle, and decay. But the living Christ endures. We must not attempt to freeze his message into forms determined by past conditions. But he himself through his Spirit will continue to generate new and authentic forms of Christian testimony. And Christ will continue to be "the way, and the truth, and the life" (John 14:6).

NOTES

[1]Stanley J. Grenz, "Postmodernism and the Future of Evangelical Theology," *Evangelical Review of Theology* 18-4 (1994): 327.

[2]For instance, see Plato's "Phaedo" in Stephen M. Cahn, ed., *Classics of Western Philosophy*, 2d ed. (Indianapolis IN: Hackett Publishing Co., 1985) 66-111; or Rene Descartes, "Meditations on First Philosophy" in Cahn, ed., 301-41.

[3]For instance, see A. J. Ayer, *The Foundations of Empirical Knowledge* (London: Macmillan and Co., 1940) or *Logical Positivism* (Glencoe IL: The Free Press, 1957); or Bertrand Russell, *An Inquiry into Meaning and Truth* (New York: W. W. Norton, 1940) or *The Problem of Philosophy* (New York: Oxford University Press, 1959).

[4]R. Albert Mohler, Jr., "Ministry Is Stranger Than It Used to Be: The Challenge of Postmodernism," *The Tie* 65-2 (1997): 4.

[5]For instance, consider the metamorphosis of the word "gay" within the last generation from its generic meaning of "lighthearted," "frivolous," "happy" to its ironic and almost exclusive association in contemporary American culture with homosexual identity and lifestyle. Thus, even the iconoclastic Friedrich Nietzsche finds his use of the term a century ago in *The Gay Science* (New York: Vintage Books, 1974) freighted today with originally undreamed-of ambiguity and double entendre.

[6]John W. Cooper, "Reformed Apologetics and the Challenge of Postmodern Relativism," *Calvin Theological Journal* 28-1 (1993): 108.

[7]Ted Peters, *God—The World's Future: Systematic Theology for a Postmodern Era* (Minneapolis: Fortress Press, 1992) 9ff.

[8]See Descartes, "Meditation One: Concerning Those Things That Can Be Called into Doubt" in "Meditations on First Philosophy."

[9]To be sure, Descartes did ground his certainty in the accuracy of the self-conscious self's analysis of reality in his belief in God. An all-good, all-knowing God is the guarantor of human reason's deliberations, since He is its creator (see Descartes, "Meditation Three: Concerning God, That He Exists," in "Meditations on First Philosophy"). For later, secular modern thinkers, reason continues its role as autonomous arbiter without the presence of God the guarantor.

[10]See Immanuel Kant, *Critique of Pure Reason* (New York: St. Martin's Press, 1965). Kant is difficult to understand, but a brief synopsis of his understanding of "pure concepts of the reason" or "transcendental ideas" can be found in *Critique of Pure Reason*, 315-22.

[11]See Friederich Schleiermacher, *The Christian Faith* (New York: Harper & Row, 1963). Schleiermacher's programmatic understanding of Christian doctrines as expressions of religious self-consciousness is set forth in chapter 1, pp. 15-17, 76-93.

[12]Examples of this type of biblically-based theology at its most sophisticated would include the works of Carl F. H. Henry, *God, Revelation, and Authority*, 4 vols. (Waco TX: Word Books, 1976-79) and Thomas F. Torrance, *Theological Science* (New York: Oxford University Press, 1969). A less technical rendering of this type of theology can be found in the works of C. S. Lewis, such as *Mere Christianity* (New York: Macmillan, 1952).

[13]These writers are notoriously difficult. Frege's writings are contained in Peter Geach and Max Black, eds., *Translations from the Philosophical Writings of Gottlebe Frege*, 2d ed. (1960). For Peirce's writings, see Charles Hartshorne, Paul Weiss, and Arthur W. Burke, eds., *The Peirce Papers: Collected Papers*, 8 vols. (1931-58). For the more accessible writings of Russell, see note 3 above.

[14]Susan Brooks Thistlethwaite, "Christology and Postmodernism," *Interpretation* LXIX-3 (1995): 270.

¹⁵See Immanuel Kant, *Grounding for the Metaphysics of Morals* (Indianapolis IN: Hackett Publishing Co., 1981) 24-30.

¹⁶Charles E. Winquist, "The Silence of the *Real*: Theology at the End of the Twentieth Century," in Robert P. Scharlemann, ed., *Theology at the End of the Century: A Dialogue on the Postmodern* (Charlottesville VA: University Press of Virginia, 1990) 37.

¹⁷Mark C. Taylor, *Erring: A Postmodern A/Theology* (Chicago: University of Chicago Press, 1984) 137.

¹⁸Winquist, "The Silence of the *Real*," 37.

¹⁹Think, for example, of Abraham's faith-laden reply to Isaac: "God himself will provide the lamb for a burnt offering, my son" (Gen 22:8). Abraham never "arrived" at his ultimate destination, but as he continued on in faith, "he looked forward to the city that has foundations, whose architect and builder is God" (Heb 11:10). Jesus himself, amidst great danger and uncertainty, "set his face to go to Jerusalem" (Luke 9:51), convinced of God's providential oversight of his way.

²⁰Taylor, *Erring*, 150.

²¹Ibid.

²²Schleiermacher describes this "feeling of absolute dependence" in *The Christian Faith*, chapter 1, pp. 4, 12-18. By "feeling," Schleiermacher does not mean an *emotion*, but rather a fundamental experience of not being self-derived or self-explanatory, but rather grounded in some greater reality. This is sort of a *subjective* twist on the proofs-of-God tradition—God as the first cause or uncaused cause—represented by St. Thomas Aquinas and a host of premodern thinkers.

²³Paul Tillich, *Systematic Theology*, Vol. 2, *Existence and the Christ* (Chicago: University of Chicago Press, 1957). See especially Part III, I, C, "The Marks of Man's Estrangement and the Concept of Sin," 44-59, and Part III, II, B, "The New Being in Jesus as the Christ," 118-38.

²⁴See St. Augustine's *Confessions* in *Great Books of the Western World*, vol. 18 (Chicago: University of Chicago Press, 1952) Book I.1.1. Compare Ps 42:1.

²⁵Mark C. Taylor, "Nothing Ends Nothing," in Scharlemann, ed., *Theology at the End of the Century*, 72.

²⁶David Ray Griffin, *God and Religion in the Postmodern World* (Albany NY: State University of New York Press, 1989) 20.

²⁷Taylor, *Erring*, 172.

²⁸Ibid.

²⁹Winfried Corduan, "An Explanation of Postmodernism and What It Means for Ministers," *The Tie* 65-2 (1997) 14.

³⁰John D. Caputo, ed., *Deconstruction in a Nutshell: A Conversation with Jacques Derrida* (New York: Fordham University Press, 1997) 31.

³¹Ibid.

³²Diogenes Allen, "Christianity and the Creed of Postmodernism," *Christian Scholars Review* XXIII-2 (1993): 122.

[33]See, for example, John B. Cobb, Jr., *Christ in a Pluralistic Age* (Philadelphia: Westminster Press, 1975), especially 31-43, 190-202.

[34]Allen, "Christianity and the Creed of Postmodernism," 123.

[35]See, for example, Andrew Sung Park's reexamination of the Christian doctrine of sin through the lens of the Korean experience of *han* ("woundedness") in *The Wounded Heart of God* (Nashville: Abingdon Press, 1993).

[36]See, for example, Emil Brunner, *The Christian Doctrine of Creation and Redemption: Dogmatics, Vol. II* (Philadelphia: Westminster Press, 1952) especially 55-61.

[37]Peters, *God—The World's Future*, 28.

[38]Ibid., xi.

[39]Caputo, ed., *Deconstruction in a Nutshell*, 22.